VIVA MOZART

VIVA MOZART

An Anthology of Appreciation

Compiled & Edited
by
GEORGE D. SNELL

AMADEUS PUBLISHING COMPANY
San Jose, California

© 1989 by George D. Snell
All Rights Reserved

Library of Congress Card Number: 88-83246

International Standard Book Number:
Paperback: 0-9621624-0-X
Hardcover: 0-9621624-1-8

Printed and bound in the United States of America by
The CAXTON PRINTERS, Ltd.
Caldwell, Idaho   83605
150502

TABLE OF CONTENTS

The Appreciators

	Page
HENRI FREDERIC AMIEL	69
GEORGE ANTHEIL	164
VLADIMIR ASHKENAZY	190
W. H. AUDEN	166
PAUL and EVA BADURA-SKODA	181
BELA BARTOK	146
JACQUES BARZUN	167
LUDWIG VAN BEETHOVEN	12
ARNOLD BENNETT	129
ALBAN BERG	153
HECTOR BERLIOZ	35
LEONARD BERNSTEIN	176
GEORGES BIZET	82
JOHANNES BRAHMS	79
BENJAMIN BRITTEN	169
FERRUCCIO BUSONI	125
ERNEST CHAUSSON	103
MARIA LUIGI CARLO CHERUBINI	10
FREDERIC CHOPIN	46
DOMENICO CIMAROSA	8
MUZIO CLEMENTI	10
AARON COPLAND	165
LORENZO DA PONTE	8
EUGENE DELACROIX	34
FREDERIC DELIUS	118
EMILY DICKINSON	76

TABLE OF CONTENTS

	Page
GAETANO DONIZETTI	33
ANTONIN DVORAK	91
EDWARD ELGAR	110
GABRIEL URBAIN FAURE	103
RUDOLF FIRKUSNY	179
EDWARD FITZGERALD	45
MIKHAIL GLINKA	43
JOHANN WOLFGANG VON GOETHE	5
CHARLES GOUNOD	64
PERCY GRAINGER	118
EDVARD GRIEG	94
CHARLES T. GRIFFES	152
THOMAS HARDY	84
JOHANN ADOLF HASSE	1
FRANZ JOSEPH HAYDN	2
HERMANN HESSE	141
E. T. A. HOFFMANN	18
GUSTAV HOLST	131
VLADIMIR HOROWITZ	165
CHARLES IVES	135
HENRY JAMES	99
RANDALL JARRELL	171
JOSEPH JOACHIM	77
JOHN KEATS	29
SOREN KIERKEGAARD	61
ZOLTAN KODALY	151
SIDNEY LANIER	92
ERICH LEINSDORF	168
FRANZ LISZT	53
EDWARD MACDOWELL	117
GUSTAV MAHLER	112

TABLE OF CONTENTS

	Page
FELIX MENDELSSOHN	43
YEHUDI MENUHIN	173
DARIUS MILHAUD	158
PIERRE MONTEUX	137
OTTO NIKOLAI	50
IGNACE JAN PADEREWSKI	115
THOMAS LOVE PEACOCK	24
SERGEI PROKOFIEV	155
GIACOMO PUCCINI	112
MARCEL PROUST	130
NIKOLAI RIMSKY-KORSAKOV	101
ROMAIN ROLLAND	127
CHARLES ROSEN	185
GIACCHINO ROSSINI	27
ANTON RUBINSTEIN	72
CAMILLE SAINT-SAENS	81
ARTUR SCHNABEL	149
ARNOLD SCHOENBERG	132
FRANZ SCHUBERT	30
ROBERT SCHUMANN	47
ALBERT SCHWEITZER	136
ROGER SESSIONS	160
GEORGE BERNARD SHAW	105
VINCENT SHEEAN	161
JEAN SIBELIUS	123
BEDRICH SMETANA	70
STENDAHL	18
WALLACE STEVENS	145
RICHARD STRAUSS	119
IGOR STRAVINSKY	147
SIR ARTHUR SULLIVAN	93

TABLE OF CONTENTS

	Page
WILLIAM MAKEPEACE THACKERAY	50
VIRGIL THOMSON	159
LEO N. TOLSTOY	71
PETER ILYITCH TSCHAIKOVSKY	85
IVAN TURGENEV	67
GIUSEPPI VERDI	64
COUNT FERDINAND WALDSTEIN	11
RICHARD WAGNER	54
BRUNO WALTER	138
CARL MARIA VON WEBER	25
REBECCA WEST	157
AVE ATQUE VALE	192

PREFACE

The plan of this book is chronological—the 'appreciators' are listed beginning with the earliest and ending with the modern. In most cases the commentaries are self-explanatory, but some information is provided that may add clarification.

Obviously another volume could be put together with still other sets of equally valid contributions because literature on the subject is so vast; however, the consensus of any other group doubtless would be little different.

Thanks are due to many who have helped in the preparation of this material—most especially my grandsons Steven and Gregory Snell; also Daniel Dixon at the University of California, Berkeley; owners of copyrights; and permissions directors of the publishing houses acknowledged herein.

Drawing by M. Stevens; © 1979 The New Yorker Magazine, Inc.

FOREWORD

If Wolfgang Amadeus Mozart had lived a long life, enjoyed international acclaim and died in affluence, interest in his career would probably be on a par with that generated by Haydn's. But there is the phenomenon of the supreme genius in music never having received a tithe of proper recognition in his lifetime. Ironically two hundred years after his death he has won a secure place in the hearts of the public and of most practioners of his art; and if fees could be collected for performances of his works, Mozart's estate would run into the multi-millions.

Yet in Mozart's lifetime his operas and symphonies were known and performed; just before his death he stood on the threshold of financial success. If he had lived only another decade, the story of his life would have been very different.

The esteem in which his work was held by those competent to appreciate it is well known. Haydn's comment to Leopold Mozart, "I, as an honest man, tell you before God that your son is the greatest composer I know in person or by name," is probably the most familiar. But what have other and later judges said? In fact a whole literature of appreciation has come into being, and not alone from other composers but from eminent persons who love music and can adequately express their verdicts. Indeed there is hardly one master among the many later artists who had nothing to say about Mozart. What other musicians have said or written throws the clearest light on his genius, makes us see what his music meant to them, and helps us respond most fully to it.

Lengthy immersion in the works of other composers can be tiring. The music of Mozart does not tire, and this is one of its miracles. Under its seeming simplicity and order lurk depths that even repeated hearing and study do not fathom. Attempting to reduce to words the effect of such music may be a futile effort, but if it can be done, surely lovers of Mozart want to know. Why, of all composers' music, does Mozart's inspire such dedicated interest, and even fanatical devotion? For one thing, it exists in almost Protean form. Every genre known to his time is present, each in perfection. In every class it has not one or two, but many examples: 21 piano sonatas, 27 piano concertos, 41 symphonies, 18 masses large and small, 13 operas, 9 oratorios and cantatas, 2 ballets, over 40 concertos for a variety of instruments, including the horn, flute and harp, organ, clarinet, oboe, violin and bassoon, not to mention the string quartets, trios and quintets, violin and piano duets, piano quartets, and the songs. In all, 626 compositions survive. We know that many were lost. This astounding output includes hardly one work less than a masterpiece.

In spite of the apparent perfection (autographs bear relatively few emendations), the labor of this production, along with the debilities caused by boyhood diseases aggravated by incessant travel as a child prodigy and the highly unsanitary conditions

FOREWORD xiii

of the 18th century—all must have contributed to Mozart's early death.

So, to go back, there is something indefinable about Mozart's music, and it has been variously called 'simple, deep;' 'angelic, demonic;' 'facile, inspired;' 'easy, difficult;'—almost every opposite in the language. David D. Boyden tells of an explorer among Indians in South America who "found that a Mozart symphony played on a portable phonograph was an *open sesame* to them. The Indians were indifferent to Sousa's *Stars and Stripes Forever* and to Louis Armstrong, but they were mad about Mozart."* At the same time, sophisticated composers have wrestled with their muses in attempts to produce sounds as profound.

The combination of 'pure' melody and ideal 'voice' must be a further contribution to this music's attractiveness. All we can say is that what has been called Mozartian is the essence of this wonderful listening pleasure. We arrive at the impasse: words cannot express the feeling music inspires. We know that in Mozart the feeling is supreme. Listening to Mozart, we cannot think of any possible improvement. Later composers with different orchestral forces and other examples for models have produced great effects, but few (Schubert perhaps excepted) have had the equal gift of creating sounds that delight, inspire, purify, bring joy or sorrow to the human soul.

Studies and interpretations of Mozart are legion.

---

*Quoted in *A Guide to Orchestral Music: the handbook for Non-Musicians* by Ethan Mordden.

Whole libraries are built upon the miracle of this man. In the following pages no attempt is made to trace the detail of his life, incidents relating to creation of his works, or any of the lore that has grown up about him, and certainly no analysis of his music in the technical sense. Here though are many anecdotes and sidelights; they are inherent in the appreciation and round out the observations of the tellers. The claim implicit in this book is that it throws a newly authentic light, by minds best fitted to train that light, on a genius in whom interest will not die as long as western culture itself survives. — G. D. S.

ACKNOWLEDGMENTS

The editor gratefully acknowledges permission to reprint copyright material. Every effort has been made to contact copyright holders but in some cases to no avail. The publisher solicits response from any copyright holders not acknowledged below.

GEORGE ANTHEIL: From *Bad Boy of Music* by George Antheil. Quoted in Composers on Music edited by Sam Morgenstern, Pantheon Books, New York, 1956. Unable to contact the copyright owner.

W. H. AUDEN: From *W. H. Auden: a Biography* by Humphrey Carpenter. Copyright (c) 1981 by George Allen & Unwin (Publishers) Ltd., London. Reprinted by permission of Houghton Mifflin Company.

VLADIMIR ASHKENAZY: From *Great Pianists Speak for Themselves* by Elyse Mach. Copyright (c) 1980 by Dodd, Mead & Company, Inc., New York. Reprinted by permission of Dodd, Mead & Company, Inc.

BELA BARTOK: From *The Life and the Music of Bela Bartok* by Halsey Stevens. Copyright (c) 1953, 1964 by Oxford University Press, Inc.; renewed 1981 by Halsey Stevens. Reprinted by permission of Oxford University Press, Inc.

JACQUES BARZUN: From *The Pleasures of Music* (1951) by Jacques Barzun. Viking Press, New York. Reprinted by permission of Jacques Barzun.

PAUL and EVA BADURA-SKODA: From *Interpreting Mozart on the Keyboard* by Paul and Eva Badura-Skoda. St. Martin's Press, New York, 1962. Reprinted by permission of Eva Badura-Skoda.

LUDWIG VAN BEETHOVEN: From *The Letters of Beethoven* edited and translated by Emily Anderson. By permission of Emily Anderson and Macmillan Publishers, Ltd., London, 1961. And from *Thayer's Life of Beethoven*, revised and edited by Elliot Forbes. Copyright 1949 (c) 1964, revised edition 1967 by Princeton University Press, Princeton, New Jersey. Reprinted by permission of Princeton University Press.

ARNOLD BENNETT: From *The Journal of Arnold Bennett*, Viking Press, New York, 1932.

ALBAN BERG: From *Life and Work of Alban Berg* by Willi Reich, translated by Cornelius Cardew. Copyright 1965 by Thames & Hudson, Ltd., London. Reprinted by permission of Thames & Hudson, Ltd.

HECTOR BERLIOZ: From *Memoirs of Hector Berlioz: from 1803 1865* by Hector Berlioz, translated by Rachel and Eleanor Holmes, annotations

ACKNOWLEDGMENTS

and revisions of translation by Ernest Newman. Copyright 1932 by Alfred A. Knopf, Inc. and renewed 1960 by Vera Newman. Reprinted by permission of Alfred A. Knopf, Inc.

LEONARD BERNSTEIN: From *The Infinite Variety of Music* by Leonard Bernstein. Simon & Schuster, New York, 1962. Copyright (c) 1966 by the Leonard Bernstein Foundation. Reprinted by permission of Simon & Schuster, Inc.

GEORGE BIZET: From *Bizet and His World* by Mina Curtiss. Alfred A. Knopf, Inc., New York, 1958. Copyright (c) Alfred A. Knopf, Inc. Reprinted by permission of Alfred A. Knopf, Inc.

BENJAMIN BRITTEN: From *Benjamin Britten, His Life and Operas* by Eric Walter White. Faber and Faber, London, 1983. Reprinted by permission of Faber and Faber Limited Publishers, London. And from *Britten* by Imogen Holst. Thomas Y. Crowell Co., New York, 1966. Unable to locate copyright owner.

FERRUCCIO BUSONI: From *The Sackbut*. Curwen & Sons, 1921, and quoted in *Mozart in Retrospect* by A. Hyatt King. Oxford University Press, London, 1955. Reprinted by permission of Mr. A. Hyatt King.

ERNEST CHAUSSON: From *Ernest Chausson: the Composer's Life and Works* by Jean-Pierre Barricelli and Leo Weinstein. Copyright (c) 1955 by the University of Oklahoma Press.

MARIA LUIGI CARLO CHERUBINI: From *Cherubini Memorials* by Edward Bellasis. Burns and Oates, 1874.

FREDERIC CHOPIN: From *The Life and Death of Chopin* by Casimir Wierzynski. Simon & Schuster, Inc. N. Y., 1949. Reprinted by permission of Simon & Schuster, Inc., New York. And from *Chopin: the Man and His Music* by Herbert Weinstock. Alfred A. Knopf, Inc., New York, 1949. Copyright (c) Alfred A. Knopf, Inc. Reprinted by permission of Alfred A. Knopf, Inc.

DOMENICO CIMAROSA: From *Mozart in Retrospect* by A. Hyatt King. Oxford University Press, London, 1955. Reprinted by permission of Mr. A. Hyatt King.

MUZIO CLEMENTI: From *Mozart in Retrospect* by A. Hyatt King. Oxford University Press, London, 1955. Reprinted by permission of Mr. A. Hyatt King.

AARON COPLAND: From *A Modernist Defends Modern Music* by Aaron Copland. Quoted in *Composers on Music* edited by Sam Morgenstern. Pantheon Books, New York, 1956. Copyright (c) 19XX by the New York Times Company. Reprinted by permission.

LORENZO DA PONTE: From *Memoirs of Lorenzo Da Ponte* edited by Arthur Livingston. J. B. Lippincott Co., Philadelphia, 1929.

ACKNOWLEDGMENTS xvii

FREDERIC DELIUS: From *Frederic Delius* by Peter Warlock. Oxford University Press, New York, 1952, and The Bodley Head, London. Reprinted by permission of Oxford University Press, London.

EUGENE DELACROIX: From *The Pleasures of Music* by Jacques Barzun. Viking Press, New York. 1951. Reprinted by permission of Jacques Barzun.

EMILY DICKINSON: From *The Poems of Emily Dickinson*. Reprinted by permission of the publishers and the Trustees of Amherst College from *The Poems of Emily Dickinson*, edited by Thomas H. Johnson, Cambridge, Mass.: The Belknap Press of Harvard University Press, Copyright 1951, (c) 1955, 1979, 1983 by the President and Fellows of Harvard College.

GAETANO DONIZETTI: From *Donizetti* by William Ashbrook, Cassell, London, 1956. Reprinted by permission of Macmillan Publishing Company. New York.

ANTONIN DVORAK: From *Dvorak* by John Clapham, as quoted in the New York Herald in 1884 now in the public domain.

SIR EDWARD ELGAR: From *Edward Elgar, His Life and Music* by Diana McVeagh. J. M. Dent & Sons, Ltd., Publishers, London, 1955. Reprinted by permission of Diana McVeagh and the Elgar Trust.

RUDOLF FIRKUSNY: From *Great Pianists Speak for Themselves* by Elyse Mach. Copyright (c) 1980 by Dodd, Mead & Company, Inc., New York. Reprinted by permission of Dodd, Mead & Company, Inc.

EDWARD FITZGERALD: From *With Friends Possessed - a Life of Edward FitzGerald* by Robert Bernard Martin. Atheneum Publishers, Inc. New York, 1985. Copyright (c) 1985 Robert Bernard Martin. Reprinted with the permission of Atheneum Publishers, an imprint of Macmillan Publishing Company.

MIKHAIL GLINKA: From *Memoirs* by Mikhail Ivanovich Glinka, translated from the Russian by Richard B. Mudge. Copyright (c) 1963 by the University of Oklahoma Press. Reprinted by permission of the University of Oklahoma Press.

JOHANN WOLFGANG VON GOETHE: From *Mozart in Retrospect* by A. Hyatt King. Oxford University Press, London, 1955. Reprinted by permission of Mr. A. Hyatt King and from *Goethe-His Life and Times* by Richard Friedenthal, World Publishing Co., New York, 1965.

CHARLES GOUNOD: From *Composers on Music*, edited by Sam Morgenstern. Quotation in Public Domain.

EDVARD GRIEG ROM *Composers of Yesterday* by David Ewen. H. W. Wilson Company, New York, 1937. Reprinted by Permission of the H. W. Wilson Company New York. And from *Edvard Grieg* by David

ACKNOWLEDGMENTS

Monrad-Johansen, translated by Madge Robertson. Princeton University Press, Princeton, New Jersey, 1938 (unable to find copyright owner).

CHARLES T. GRIFFES: From *Charles T. Griffes: the Life of an American Composer* by Edward M. Maisel. Alfred A. Knopf, New York, 1943. Copyright by Alfred A. Knopf, Inc. (c) 1943. Reprinted by permission of Alfred A. Knopf, Inc.

THOMAS HARDY: From *The Complete Poems of Thomas Hardy* edited by James Gibson. Macmillan, New York, 1978. Reprinted by permission of Macmillan Publishing Company, a division of Macmillan, Inc.

JOHANN ADOLF HASSE: From *Letters of Composers* edited by Norman and Shrifte. Alfred A. Knopf, New York, 1946. Unable to locate copyright owner (Gertrude Norman).

FRANZ JOSEPH HAYDN: From *Haydn, a Creative Life in Music* by Karl Geiringer. University of California Press, Berkeley and Los Angeles, 3rd Edition, 1982. And from *Composers on Music* edited by Sam Morgenstern, Pantheon Books, New York, 1956. And from *Haydn* by H. E. Jacob, Rinehart & Co., New York, 1950.

HERMANN HESSE: From *Steppenwolf* by Hermann Hesse, translated by Basil Creighton. Copyright 1929, (c) 1957 by Holt, Rinehart and Winston. Reprinted by permission of Henry Holt and Company, Inc.

E. T. A. HOFFMAN: From *Mozart in Retrospect* by A. Hyatt King. Oxford University Press, London, 1955. Reprinted by permission of Mr. A. Hyatt King.

GUSTAV HOLST: From *Gustav Holst* by Imogen Holst. Oxford University Press, New York. 1938. And from *The Heritage of Music* by Gustav Holst. Oxford University Press, London. 1927.

CHARLES E. IVES: From *Charles E. Ives: Memos*, edited by John Kirkpatrick. Copyright (c) 1972 by W. W. Norton & Company, Inc. Reprinted by permission of W. W. Norton & Company, Inc.

RANDALL JARRELL: From *The Complete Poems* ("The Augsburg Adoration"). Copyright (c) 1945, 1965 by Mrs. Randall Jarell, copyright renewed 1968, 1969 by Mrs. Randall Jarell. Reprinted by permission of Farrar, Straus and Giroux, Inc.

JOHN KEATS: From *Complete Works of John Keats* edited by H. B. Forman, London, 1911.

SOREN KIERKEGAARD: From "Either/Or" in *A Kierkegaard Anthology* edited by Robert Bretall. Random House, New York, 1936. Copyright 1946 (c) renewed by Princeton University Press. Reprinted by permission of Princeton University Press.

A. HYATT KING: From *Mozart in Retrospect* by A. Hyatt King. Copyright

ACKNOWLEDGMENTS xix

right (c) by A. Hyatt King. Oxford University Press, London, 1955. Reprinted by permission of A. Hyatt King.

ZOLTAN KODALY: From *The Selected Writings of Zoltan Kodaly*. Boosey & Hawkes, Ltd., London 1974. Reprinted by permission of Boosey & Hawkes Music Publishers, Ltd.

SIDNEY LANIER: From *The Pleasure of Music* by Jacques Barzun. The Viking Press, New York, 1951. Reprinted by permission of Jacques Barzun.

ERICH LEINSDORF: From *Cadenza* by Erich Leinsdorf. Copyright (c) 1976 by Erich Leinsdorf. Reprinted by permission of Houghton Mifflin Company. And from an interview in the San Jose Mercury, January 24, 1984.

FRANZ LISZT: From *The Letters of Franz Liszt* translated and edited by Howard E. Hugo. Harvard University Press, Cambridge, 1953. Reprinted by permission of Harvard University Press.

GUSTAV MAHLER: From *Recollections of Gustav Mahler* by Natalie Bauer-Lechner, Cambridge University Press, N. Y., 1980. Reprinted with the permission of Cambridge University Press. And from *Gustav Mahler and Guido Adler* edited by Edward Reilly, Cambridge University Press, N. Y., 1982. Reprinted with the permission of Cambridge University Press. And from *Gustav Mahler - Memories and Letters* edited by Donald Mitchell. Viking Press, New York, 1946. Copyright by John Murray (Publihers) Ltd., London. Reprinted by permission of John Murray (Publishers) Ltd.

FELIX MENDELSSOHN: From *Letters of Felix Mendelssohn* edited by Gisele Seldon-Goth. Pantheon Books, New York, 1945. Copyright (c) Pantheon Books. Reprinted by permission of Pantheon Books, a Division of Random House, Inc. And from *The Musician's World* edited by Hans Gals. Copyright (c) by Thames & Hudson, Ltd., London, 1965. Reprinted by permission of Thames & Hudson, Ltd.

YEHUDI MENUHIN: From *Unfinished Journey: the Autobiography of Yehudi Menuhin*. Copyright (c) by Alfred A. Knopf, Inc., New York, 1976. Reprinted by permission of Alfred A. Knopf, Inc. And from *Yehudi Menuhin* by Robert Magidoff. Copyright (c) 1955 by Robert Magidoff. Reprinted by permission of Doubleday, a division of Bantam, Doubleday, Dell Publishing Company.

DARIUS MILHAUD: From *Notes Without Music* by Darius Milhaud, translated by Donald Evans. Copyright (c) by Alfred A. Knopf, Inc. New York, 1953. Reprinted by permission of Alfred A. Knopf, Inc.

PIERRE MONTEUX: From *It's All in the Music* by Doris Monteux. Farrar, Straus and Giroux, Inc., New York, 1965. Copyright (c) 1965 by Dor-

ACKNOWLEDGMENTS

is G. Monteux. Reprinted by permission of Farrar, Straus and Giroux, Inc.

OTTO NICOLAI: From *Musical Events: A Chronicle, 1980–1983* (Summit). (c) 1980 Andrew Porter. Originally in The New Yorker.

IGNACE JAN PADEREWSKI: From *Paderewski* by Charlotte Kellogg. Copyright 1956 by Charlotte Kellogg, renewed (c) 1984 by Jean Kellogg Dickie. All rights reserved. Reprinted by permission of Viking Penguin, Inc.

THOMAS LOVE PEACOCK: From *Pleasures of Music* ed. by Jacques Barzun, New York, Viking Press, 1951.

SERGEI PROKOFIEV: From *Sergei Prokofiev* by Victor Seroff. Funk and Wagnalls company, New York, 1968. Copyright owner unknown.

MARCEL PROUST: From *Swann in Love* section of *Remembrance of Things Past*, Random House, New York, 1984.

GIACOMO PUCCINI: From *Immortal Bohemian* by Dante del Fiorentino. Prentice-Hall, New York, 1952.

NIKOLAI RIMSKY-KORSAKOV: From *My Musical Life* by Nikolai Rimsky-Korsakov, translated by Judah A. Joffe. Tudor Publishing Co., New York, 1936. Copyright (c) 1950 Alfred A. Knopf, Inc. Reprinted by permission of Alfred A. Knopf, Inc. And from *Reminiscences of Rimsky-Korsakov* by Y. V. Yastreftsev. Columbia University Press, New York, 1985. Reprinted by permission of Columbia University Press.

ROMAIN ROLLAND: From *Some Musicians of Former Days* by Romain Rolland, Henry Holt & Co., New York, 1915.

CHARLES ROSEN: From *The Classical Style* by Charles Rosen. Copyright (c) 1971 by Charles Rosen. All rights reserved. Reprinted by permission of Viking Penguin, Inc.

GIACCHINO ROSSINI: From *The Life of Rossini* by Stendahl. Translated by Richard Coe. John Calder Publishers, Ltd. London, 1970. Reprinted by permission of John Calder Publishers. Ltd. London. And from *Richard Wagner's Visit to Rossini* translated by Herbert Weinstock. University of Chicago Press, Chicago, 1968. Illustrated by Warren Chappell. Reprinted by permission of the University of Chicago Press.

CAMILLE SAINT-SAENS: From *Musical Memories of Camille Saint-Saens*, translated by Edwin Gile Rich. Small, Maynard and Company, New York. Quoted in *Composers on Music*, edited by Sam Morgenstern. Unable to locate copyright owner.

ARTUR SCHNABEL: From *Artur Schnabel* by Cesar Saerchinger. Copyright (c) by Dodd, Mead & Company, Inc., New York, 1957. Reprinted by permission of Dodd, Mead & Company, Inc.

ARNOLD SCHOENBERG: From *Schoenberg Remembered* by Dika Newlin

ACKNOWLEDGMENTS　　　　　　　　　　　　xxi

by permission of Pendragon Press, 1980, Stuyvesant, New York and from *Schoenberg and the God Idea* by Pamela C. White. UMI Research Press, Ann Arbor, Michigan, 1985.

FRANZ SCHUBERT: From *Schubert—Memories by his Friends* edited by Otto Erich Deutsch. A. & C. Black Publishers, Ltd. London, 1958. Reprinted by permission of A. & C. Black Publishers, Ltd., London. And from *Mozart in Retrospect* by A. Hyatt King. Oxford University Press, London, 1955. Reprinted by permission of Mr. A. Hyatt King. And from *The Schubert Reader* by Otto Erich Deutsch. W. W. Norton & Company, Inc., 1947. Reprinted by permission of W. W. Norton & Company, Inc.

ROBERT SCHUMANN: From *The Musical World of Robert Schumann* by Henry Pleasants. St. Martin's Press, New York, 1965. Reprinted by permission of Henry Pleasants. And from *The Pleasures of Music* by Jacques Barzun. The Viking Press, New York, 1951. Reprinted by permisssion of Jacques Barzun.

ALBERT SCHWEITZER: From *Music in the Life of Albert Schweitzer* by Charles R. Joy. Harper & Row, New York, Copyright (c) Harper & Row. Reprinted by permission of Harper & Row Publishers, Inc., New York.

ROGER SESSIONS: From *The Musical Experience of Composer, Performer, Listener*. Copyright 1950 (c) by Princeton University Press. Reprinted by permission of Princeton University Press.

GEORGE BERNARD SHAW: From *To a Young Actress . . . letters to Molly Tompkins*. Clarkson N. Potter, New York, 1960. Reprinted by permission of The Society of Authors, London. And from *Shaw, An Autobiography*. Weybright & Talley, New York, 1969. Reprinted by permission of The Society of Authors, London. And from *The Great Composers* by Bernard Shaw., edited by Louis Crompton. University of California Press, Berkeley, 1978. Reprinted by permission of The Society of Authors, London, on behalf of the Bernard Shaw Estate. And from *Pleasures of Music* by Jacques Barzun. The Viking Press, New York, 1951. Reprinted by permission of Mr. Jacques Barzun and from *Bernard Shaw-Collected Letters 1898–1910* ed. by Dan H. Laurence, Dodd, Mead & Co., New York, 1972.

VINCENT SHEEAN: From *First and Last Love* by Vincent Sheean. Copyright (c) 1956 by Vincent Sheean. Reprinted by permission of Random House, Inc., New York.

JEAN SIBELIUS: From *Jean Sibelius* by Karl Ekman, translated by Edward Birse. Tudor Publishing Company, New York, 1945. Copyright (c) by Alfred A. Knopf, Inc. 1938. Reprinted by permission of Watkins/

ACKNOWLEDGMENTS

Loomis Agency, Inc., New York and from *The Music of Jean Sibelius* by Burnett James. Fairleigh Dickinson University Press, 1983.

SOUTH AMERICAN INDIANS: From *A Guide to Orchestral Music: the Handbook for Non-Musicians* by Ethan Mordden. Copyright (c) 1980 by Ethan Mordden. Reprinted by permission of Oxford University Press, Inc.

STENDAHL HENRI BEYLE: From *The Private Diaries of Stendahl* translated and edited by Robert Sage. Copyright (c) 1958 by Robert Sage. Reprinted by permission of Doubleday, a division of Bantam, Doubleday, Dell Publishing Group, Inc.

WALLACE STEVENS: From *The Collected Poems of Wallace Stevens*. Alfred A. Knopf, New York, 1980. Copyright by Alfred A. Knopf, Inc. Reprinted by permission of Alfred A. Knopf, Inc.

RICHARD STRAUSS: From *Betrachtungen und Erinnerungen* by Richard Strauss. Reprinted by permission of Boosey & Hawkes, Inc. New York, as quoted in *Composers of Music* by Sam Morgenstern. Pantheon Books. New York, 1956 and from *Richard Strauss* by Norman Del Mar. Chilton Book Co., New York, 1969.

IGOR STRAVINSKY: From *Retrospects and Conclusions* by Igor Stravinsky and Robert Craft. Copyright (c) 1969 by Alfred A. Knopf, Inc., New York. Reprinted by permission of Alfred A. Knopf, Inc.

SIR ARTHUR SULLIVAN: From *Sir Arthur Sullivan* by Herbert Sullivan and Newman Flower. Cassell & Co., Ltd. London, 1950. Reprinted by permission of Macmillan Publishing Company, N. Y.

VIRGIL THOMSON: From *Virgil Thomson* by Virgil Thomson. Copyright (c) 1966 by Alfred A. Knopf, Inc., New York. Reprinted by permission of Alfred A. Knopf, Inc.

TSCHAIKOVSKY PETER ILYITCH: From *Tschaikovsky - The Diaries*. Translated by Vladimir Lakond. W. W. Norton & Company, New York, 1945.

GIUSEPPI VERDI: From *Composers on Music* by Sam Morgenstern. Pantheon Books, New York, 1956. Excerpt from Verdi letter to Clarina Maffei copyrighted by Alma Mahler-Werfel.

RICHARD WAGNER: From *Cosima Wagner's Diaries Volume 1, 1869 1877*, edited by Martin Grego-Dellin and Dietrich Mack, copyright (c) 1976 by R. Piper & Co. Verlag; English translation copyright (c) 1978, 1977 by Geoffrey Skelton and Harcourt Brace Jovanovich, Inc. Reprinted by permission of Harcourt Brace Jovanovich, Inc. And from *Opera and Drama* by Richard Wagner, 1851.

BRUNO WALTER: From *Music and Music-Making* by Bruno Walter, translated by Paul Hamburger. Reprinted by permission of W. W. Norton & Company, Inc. Copyright (c) 1957 by Bruno Walter. Copyright

ACKNOWLEDGMENTS xxiii

renewed 1985. English translation Copyright (c) 1961 by Faber & Faber, Ltd.

CARL MARIA VON WEBER: From *Enchanted Wanderer* by Lucy Poate Stebbins. G. P. Putnam's Sons, New York, 1940. Copyright by G. P. Putnam's Sons, reprinted by permission of The Putnam Publishing Group.

REBECCA WEST: From *Black Lamb and Grey Falcon* by Rebecca West. The Viking Press, New York, 1941. Reprinted by permission of The Viking Penguin, Inc.

MINUET
Composed at the Age of Six

W. A. Mozart
(1756-1791)

VIVA MOZART

Mozart must have had days like this.

Johann Adolf Hasse

(1699–1783), born in Bergdorf, Germany, flourished in Italy as a highly admired and successful composer of *opera seria*, working with librettos by the poet Metastasio. His forte was *bel canto* music in which he was unexcelled in his day. He lived long enough to see his prophecy about Mozart fulfilled; by the year of his death, the masterpieces *Idomeneo* (1781), *The Abduction from the Seraglio* (1782) and the *Haffner Symphony* (1782) had already been performed to great applause.

Vienna, September 30, 1769
To the Abbe Giovanni Maria Ortes

I have made the acquaintance here of a certain Herr Mozart (Leopold), Kappellmeister to the Archbishop of Salzburg, a clever man, charming and cultivated, who, I believe, knows his business in music as well as other matters. He has a daughter and a son. The former plays the cembalo proficiently, and the latter, who cannot be more than twelve or thirteen years old, already holds forth as a composer and teacher of music.

I have seen the compositions he is supposed to have written. They are not at all bad and I should not have recognized in them a twelve-year-old author. I dare not question his having written them, for after giving me proof of various styles on the cembalo, he showed me some things which were incredible for that age and admirable even for a grown man.

Since his father wishes to take him to Italy to make him known and wrote me requesting some letters of recommendation, I am taking the liberty of sending you one. I am depending on your kindness. The sole purpose of this letter is to have him meet you and to have him obtain some useful advice which may prove necessary in that country. But if you could also introduce him to some lady of your acquaintance, that would be more than I had hoped for. The father says he will leave Salzburg on October 24 and should arrive by the end of the month.

This Herr Mozart is an extremely courteous and gracious man, and his children are very well bred. The boy, more-over, is handsome, lively, charming, and has excellent manners. I am certain that if he continues to progress as he grows older, he will be a prodigy—provided the father does not push him too much and spoil him with undue and exaggerated praise, which is the one thing I dread. . . .

J. A. Hasse

From "Letters of Composers" edited by Norman and Shrifte.

Franz Joseph Haydn

(1732–1809) was born in Rohan, Austria, became a chorister at St. Stephen's Cathedral, Vienna and later, at the palace of Count Morzin, began composition, among other music, of his over 100 symphonies. Then as Kapellmeister for Prince Esterhazy (1766) he produced his large output of string, piano, choral and operatic music. In 1791 (year of Mozart's death) he left for London where he wrote his most celebrated symphonies, these last works much influenced by the music of Mozart. He had met and admired the younger man in Vienna and followed his career with great interest all his life.

From a letter (December 1787) Haydn to a group of friends represented by Luigia Polzelli, asking him to write an opera:

Why should they ask (me) for an opera *so long as Mozart is alive!* Such a great master can occupy the field alone. Ah, if only I could persuade every friend of music, but especially the great ones, to understand and to feel Mozart's inimitable works as deeply as I do and to study them with as great feeling and musical understanding as I give to them. If I could, how the cities would compete to possess such peerlessness within their walls. Prague would do well to keep a firm grip upon this wonderful man—but also to reward him with treasures. For unless they are rewarded, the life of great geniuses is sorrowful and, alas, affords little encouragement to posterity to strive more nobly; for that reason so many promising spirits succumb . . . It angers me that this unique man Mozart has not yet been engaged by some imperial or royal court. Forgive me, honored sirs, for digressing, but I like the man so well . . .

A remark reported by Leopold Mozart, made by Haydn after the latter had listened to a Mozart quartet:

I, as an honest man, tell you before God that your son is the greatest composer I know in person or by name.

VIVA MOZART

A remark by Haydn to the English critic Burney, after Mozart's death:

"Believe me, I am nothing compared to Mozart!"

In a letter to Marianna Sabina von Genzinger:

"Posterity will not have another such talent in a hundred years."

In a letter to Mozart's Masonic friend Michael Puchberg; London, Jan. 1792:

For a considerable time I was utterly distraught at Mozart's death and could not believe that Providence would so soon call such an inimitable man into the other world. Above all, I regret that Mozart before his death did not have the chance to convince the English, who are still ignorant, of the truth of what I daily preach to them (Mozart's great talent). Will you, my dear friend Puchberg, have the kindness to send me a list of those works of Mozart's that are still unknown here. I shall make every effort to promote them for the benefit of his widow. I wrote to the poor woman myself three weeks ago, telling her that when her dear son reaches the proper age, I will devote all my strength to teaching him composition without fee, in order to somewhat fill the place of his father.

From Haydn, a Creative Life in Music *by Karl Geiringer:*

After the Vienna premiere of *Don Giovanni*, sundry passages were criticized in his (Haydn's) presence and he exclaimed: "I cannot settle this dispute but this I know: Mozart is the greatest composer that the world possesses now."

JOHANN WOLFGANG VON GOETHE

(1749–1832) was born in Frankfurt, studied law at the University of Leipzig, but his leanings toward a literary career soon found fruition in a drama, likely inspired by his discovery of Shakespeare, *Gotz von Berlichingen* (1773). He met Schiller in 1794, another stimulus; and in ensuing years he was recognized as Germany's greatest man of letters. His masterpieces, *Wilhelm Meister* (1796) and *Faust* (1808) are monuments in world literature.

From "Letters to Eckermann" by Goethe (18——):

"I was only fourteen years old, but I see, as if I were still there (in Frankfurt), the little man (Mozart) with his child's sword and his curly hair . . . A phenomenon like that of Mozart remains an inexplicable thing."

From "Mozart in Retrospect" by A. Hyatt King:

Goethe divined the universality of Mozart's genius and the prophetic quality of his late works, especially *Die Zauberflote*. In 1829 he said that Mozart represented 'something unattainable in music, even as Shakespeare does in poetry.' He found in him 'a latent, procreative force which is continuously effective from generation to generation, and is not likely soon to be exhausted.' Goethe also felt that Mozart would have been well fitted to set to music his *Faust*, whose inner meaning he compared to that of *Die Zauberflote*. . . . He believed sincerely, but surely erroneously, that Mozart at his early death had, like Raphael and Byron, (he might have added Purcell), fulfilled his mission in life.

From "Goethe - His Life and Times" by Richard Friedenthal:

On August 18, 1763, when Goethe was 14, the 7-year-old Mozart and his slightly older sister gave the first of four performances in Frankfurt. 'I still remember the little fellow quite clearly with his powdered hair and his sword,' he wrote in his old age. It was a recital of clever tricks rather than a concert; the tickets cost a *thaler*. According to the advertisement puff the boy was to 'play the most difficult pieces by the greatest masters, perform on the clavecin, violin and organ, with the keyboard covered as well, determine from a distance, with his absolute pitch, the notes sounded by bells, glasses and clocks, and exhibit an aptitude scarcely ever before seen or heard. We know how much the boy earned on these journeys all over Europe, and how dearly he had to pay for this premature exploitation.

When, in conversation with Eckermann, the talk once turned to the subject of early death, Goethe, who had survived everyone, said:

Do you know how I see it? Man must be brought

to nought again! Every exceptional person has a certain mission he is called upon to fulfill. When he has accomplished it, he is no longer needed on earth in this form, and providence makes use of him again for something else. But since here below everything happens in a natural way, the demons trip him up over and over again until finally he succumbs. Thus it was with Napoleon and many others. Mozart died in this thirty-sixth year, Raphael at about the same age, and Byron was only a little older. But all had fulfilled their missions consummately, and it was probably time for them to go, so that something should remain for other people to do in the long-destined duration of this world's existence.

From "Some Musicians of Former Days" by Romain Rolland:

On December 29, 1797, Schiller wrote to Goethe: "I had always hoped that tragedy would be evolved from opera in a finer and nobler form, as formerly it was evolved from the choruses and fetes of Bacchus. In reality, opera may avoid all servile imitation of nature; and by the power of music, by the excitation of the sensibilities that free the emotions from their coarser attributes, opera inclines the mind to the noblest feelings. Even passion itself may be shown with freedom because music accompanies it; and the wonderful, which is tolerated there, should make the spirit still less concerned with the subject."

Goethe replied: "If you could have been present at the last performance of *Don Giovanni*, you would have seen all your desires about opera realized. But that piece is unique, and Mozart's death has destroyed all hope of our ever seeing anything else like it." (December 30, 1797).

Domenico Cimarosa

(1749–1801), born in Aversa, Italy, was the son of a bricklayer. Orphaned, his youth was difficult; nevertheless, he was enrolled at the Conservatorio Santa Maria di Loreta, and when he was 23 had produced his first opera. He composed sixty-five operas earning an honored niche in Italian music. Today probably only his *Il Matrimonio Segreto* (1792) is still being regularly mounted.

From "Mozart in Retrospect" by A. Hyatt King:

It is said that Cimarosa, when flattered by a painter who told him he was greater than Mozart, retorted: "Sir, what would you say to a man who told you that you were greater than Raphael?"

Lorenzo Da Ponte

(1749–1838) was a native of Ceneda, Italy, became a school teacher at Venice before being exiled on charges of a disorderly life style. He moved to Vienna where, upon recommendation of Mazzola, he met Salieri who gained for him the post of 'theatrical poet' at the court of Emperor Joseph II. Mozart met him through Baron Wezlar, an historic moment, for Da Ponte became the librettist of *The Marriage of Figaro* (1786), *Don Giovanni* (1787) and *Cosi Fan Tutte* (1790). In his old age Da Ponte, living in New York City, published an autobiography in which he takes the lion's share of credit for the success of these great operas, but there is a preponderance of evidence that Mozart collaborated to an unusual degree on the finished librettos.

From "Memoirs of Lorenzo Da Ponte" edited by Arthur Livingston:

Before long several composers had turned to me for librettos. But there were only two in Vienna deserving of my esteem: Martini, at the time the composer most favored by Joseph II, and Wolfgang Mozart, who I had the opportunity of meeting in just those days at the house of Baron Vetzlar, his great admirer and friend. Though gifted with talents superior perhaps to those of any other composer in the world, past, present or future, Mozart had, thanks to the intrigues of his rivals, never been able to exercise his divine genius in Vienna, and was living there unknown and obscure, like a priceless jewel buried in the bowels of the earth and hiding the refulgent excellence of its splendors. I can never remember without exultation and complacency that it was to my perseverance and firmness alone that Europe and the world in great part owe the exquisite vocal compositions of that admirable genius. The unfairness and envy of journalists, gazetteers and, especially of biographers of Mozart, have never permitted them to concede such glory to an Italian; but all Vienna, all those who knew him and me in Germany, Bohemia and Saxony, all his family and more than anyone else, Baron Vetzlar, under whose roof the first scintillation of that noble flame was allowed to glow, must bear me witness to the truth which I now reveal.

Muzio Clementi

(1752–1832), born in Rome, at 10 was appointed a church organist and went on to become one of the great pianists of his day, once at Vienna pitted against Mozart in a keyboard contest, graciously acknowledging Mozart's superiority. He spent many years in London, wrote extensively for the piano and orchestra. His body lies in Westminster Abbey.

From "Mozart in Retrospect" by A. Hyatt King:

Clementi, when hearing a rehearsal of the Finale of the G minor Symphony, then recently arranged as a septet by the London publisher G. D. Cimador: "Mozart has reached the boundary gate of music, and has leapt over it, leaving behind the old masters, the moderns and posterity itself."

Maria Luigi Carlo Cherubini

(1760–1842) was born in Florence, Italy, had composed masses and cantatas by age 16, and in London at 24 the King appointed him composer to the throne. However, he moved to Paris and in 1821 became director of the Paris Conservatoire. Of his many operas only *Medea* (1797) is still being heard today.

From "Cherubini: Memorials" by Edward Bellasis:

In 1805, Cherubini, to calm his mind and dissipate his cares, undertook a labour of love in getting up a performance of Mozart's Requiem, which the Parisians had never yet heard. 'Despite the disinclination of the Parisians for German music,' said German journals of the time, 'and despite the repugnance of Parisian artists to such a difficult task, Cherubini's zeal and love for this work of Mozart enabled him to get it performed by two hundred of the best singers and instrumentalists; and performed too, in such a manner, that on the very same day he received a request to repeat it. The work, in fact, made a deep sensation; and it is interesting to know that he who led the first performance of it in Paris, was destined himself to write two Requiems, which, in the opinion of a great many, cannot be deemed inferior to that of Mozart.

It is recorded that Cherubini (once) sought Mozart's tomb, but that, on being unable to find the resting place of him for whom he had so strong and affection, felt that Vienna was not the place for him. Such neglect of honour and love for this mighty genius struck him so forcibly.

Count Ferdinand Waldstein

(1762–1823) was born in Dux, Bohemia. While serving his novitiate at Bonn in 1787 he met Beethoven. An amateur musician himself, he was so impressed that he helped the younger man with many gifts and encouragement, repaid when Beethoven dedicated to him the great *Piano Sonata in C*, Opus 53, the "Waldstein."

Quoted in "Haydn" by Karl Geiringer:

Count Waldstein wrote the following words of farewell in Beethoven's album on October 29, 1792, before the young musician's departure for Vienna (to study with Haydn):

Dear Beethoven,

You are traveling to Vienna in fulfillment of your long-cherished wish. The tutelary genius of Mozart (an admirer of Mozart's music at Waldstein's court) is still weeping and bewailing the death of her favorite. With the inexhaustible Haydn she has found a refuge, but no occupation, and she is now waiting to associate herself with someone else. Labor assiduously and receive Mozart's spirit from the hands of Haydn.

LUDWIG VAN BEETHOVEN

(1770–1827) was born in Bonn, Germany, son of a choir singer, and showed his musical ability early, appearing as a concert pianist at age 8, moved to Vienna where he played for Mozart who is said to have remarked, "Someday the world will hear of this young man." Beethoven's early works show derivatives from both Haydn and Mozart, then in a second period while suffering from deafness, his originality became manifest in the symphony (especially his 3rd, 5th and 7th), the piano sonatas and string quartets. His third period produced the great 9*th Symphony* and the last string quartets. Never marrying, he was a difficult man in social relationships but of uncompromising fidelity to his musical genius. He met Mozart only once as a young man and may have taken lessons from him.

From Carl Czerny's notes:

"In later years Beethoven also told me (Czerny) that he had often heard Mozart play and that, since in his day the invention of the Fortepiano was as yet in its infancy, Mozart had become used to playing in a manner suited to the most customary harpsichords, which was not at all suited to the Fortepiano. Afterwards I made the acquaintance of several people who had studied with Mozart and found that their way of playing fully bore out this observation.

Once, in my house, Beethoven saw the scores of the six Mozart Quartets. He opened the 5th in A (K. 464) and said, 'That is a work! In it Mozart said to the world: "See what I could create if the time had come for you!"'

From a letter to 12-year-old Emilie M. written by Beethoven from Teplitz, July 17, 1812:

"Do not snatch away the laurels from Handel, Haydn, and Mozart, for they deserve them; as yet I do not."

From "Mozart in Retrospect" by A. Hyatt King:

On hearing a performance of Mozart's C Minor Piano Concerto about the year 1800, in company with Carl Cramer, Beethoven exclaimed, "Cramer! Cramer! We shall never be able to do anything like that!"

From "The Letters of Beethoven" ed. and translated by Emily Anderson:

Letter to Brietkopf & Hartel,
Vienna, July 13, 1802.

It is my firm opinion that only Mozart could translate his own works from the piano to other instruments—Haydn like-wise—and without wishing to join company with these two great men, I believe that it is also true of my piano sonatas.

Letter, c. May, 1820, to Tobias Haslinger, Vienna—I have taken on a bet of 10 gulden V.C., I repeat ten gulden V.C., that it is not true that you have had to pay 2000 gulden as compensation to Artaria for the publication of Mozart's works (which, moreover, have already been pirated everywhere and sold in pirated copies)—I would certainly know the truth. I really cannot believe it. But if this injustice has indeed been perpetrated against you, then 'O dolce contento' I must pay the 10 gulden—... in this matter (the adding of a coda to a work of his) I am of the same opinion as some great men such as Haydn, Mozart and Cherubini who never hesitated to delete, shorten or lengthen and so on—Sapienti pauca.

Letter, February 6, 1826, to Abbe Maximilian Stadler:

You have really performed a very good deed by rendering justice to the shades of Mozart in your truly masterly work, which is such a penetrating study of the subject. (Gottfried Weber had recently published . . . an article casting doubts on the genu-

VIVA MOZART

ineness of certain obviously genuine passages in Mozart's *Requiem*. Stadler immediately defended Mozart in a monograph published in Vienna, 1826, and sent a copy to Beethoven.)

From Thayer's "Life of Beethoven" as revised and edited by Elliot Forbes:

Beethoven, who as a youth of great promise, came to Vienna in the spring of 1787, but was obliged to return to Bonn after a brief sojourn, was taken to Mozart and at that musician's request played something for him which he, taking it for granted that it was a show-piece prepared for the occasion, praised in a rather cool manner. Beethoven observing this, begged Mozart to give him a theme for improvisation. He always played admirably when excited and now he was inspired too, by the presence of the master whom he reverenced greatly; he played in such a style that Mozart, whose attention and interest grew more and more, finally went silently to some friends who were sitting in an adjoining room, and said vivaciously, 'Keep your eyes on him; some day he will give the world something to talk about.'

During Beethoven's visit to Vienna he received some instruction from Mozart, but the latter, as Beethoven lamented, never played for him. That is, during the lessons which must have been confined consequently to theory. But according to a communication from Czerny to Otto Jahn, Beethoven had explained to him that he had heard Mozart play: he had a fine but choppy (*zerhacktes*) way of playing, no *ligato*. Czerny adds that Beethoven played this way at first, treating the pianoforte like an organ. From these notices it is presumed that there was some occasion, public or private, attended by Beethoven at which Mozart performed on the piano.

"Of all composers," says Reis (Notizen, p. 84) "Beethoven valued most highly Mozart and Handel, then S. Bach. Whenever I found him with music in his hand or lying on his desk it was surely compositions of these heroes. Haydn seldom escaped without a few sly thrusts." Compare this with what Jahn heard from Czerny: "Once Beethoven saw at my house the scores of six quartets by Mozart. He opened the fifth, in A, and said: 'That's a work! that's where Mozart said to the world: Behold what I might have done for you if the time were right!'

One evening Horzalka (Johann Friedrich Horzalka (1778–1860) composer and pianist) called and found only Baroness Born there. Among other topics, Mozart came under discussion, and the Baroness asked Beethoven, in writing of course, which of Mozart's operas he thought the most of. *"Die Zauberflöte,"* said Beethoven and, suddenly clasping his hands and throwing up his eyes, exclaimed, "Oh, Mozart!" As Horzalka had, as was the custom, always considered *Don Giovanni* the greatest of Mozart's operas, this opinion by Beethoven made a very deep impression upon him.

Mr. C. Czerny—who, by-the-by, knows every note

of Beethoven by heart, though he does not play one single composition of his own without the music before him—told me (Edward Schulz, an Englishman) however, that B. was sometimes inexhaustible in his praise of Mozart.

Among Beethoven's intimate friends was Abbe Stadler, an old man and an old-fashioned musician, the horizon of whose aesthetic appreciation was marked by the death-date of his friend Mozart. Castelli says that he used to call Beethoven's music "pure nonsense"; certain it is that he used to leave the concert-room whenever a composition by Beethoven was to be played. Schuppanzigh offered as an excuse for him that he had a long way to go to get home, and it does not appear that Beethoven ever took umbrage at his conduct. Holz, telling Beethoven in February 1825 that as usual he had left the room when an overture by Beethoven was about to be played, added: "He is too old. He always says when Mozart is reached, 'More I cannot understand.'"

A letter to Abbe Stadler, February 6, 1826:

I have always counted myself among the greatest admirers of Mozart and shall remain so until my last breath—
Reverend Sir, *your blessing very soon—*
With sincere regards, venerable Sir, I remain your faithful
Beethoven

E. T. A. Hoffmann

(1776–1822) was born in Konigsberg, Germany, a writer and composer, and in some respects a precursor of Poe as the originator of fantastic tales. His opera *Undine* (1816) was initially a great success but has seldom been performed; his writings, principally reviews of his favorite composers, Haydn, Mozart and Beethoven, are still worth reading.

From "Mozart in Retrospect" by A. Hyatt King:

E. T. A. Hoffmann, who ranks . . . more as a poet than a musician, confessed that Mozart led him 'into the depth of the spirit world,' to which *Don Giovanni* above all held the key. Of the E flat symphony, which he called the 'swan song' he said: 'Love and melancholy breathe forth in purest spirit tones: we feel ourselves drawn with inexpressible longing towards the forms which beckon us to join them in their flight through the clouds to another sphere.' In September 1812 he wrote his own *Don Juan* . . . One of the most remarkable pieces of prose ever inspired by an opera, Hoffmann's imaginative interpretation of Mozart's music foreshadows the powerful appeal which it was to make to 'a generation brought up on Byronic Satanism.'

Stendahl

(pen name of Marie-Henri Beyle) (1783–1842) was born in Grenoble, France, and at the age of 16 moved to Paris, thus beginning a peripatetic life spent mostly in Italy and France. His first published book in 1814 dealt with music and composers, and his major literary work, the novel *The Red and the Black*, appeared in 1830.

From "The Red and the Black":

Chapter 6 with the motto "Non so piu cosa son,
Cosa facio.
Mozart: Figaro

As soon as Madame Derville arrived, Julien felt that she was his friend: he hastened to show her the view that was to be seen from the end of the new path; as a matter of fact it was equal, if not superior, to the most admirable scenery which Switzerland and the Italian lakes have to offer. By climbing the steep slope which began a few yards farther on, one came presently to high precipices fringed with oakwoods, which projected almost over the bed of the river. It was to the summits of these sheer rocks that Julien, happy, free, and indeed something more, lord of the house, led the two friends, and relished their admiration of those sublime prospects.

"To me it is like Mozart's music," said Madame Derville.

From "Private Diaries of Stendahl" translated and edited by Robert Sage:

It was during the twilight hours of one of these soft summer evenings (circa 1805), sitting with Minette and Strombeck at a little painted table beneath the lofty elms of Der Grune Jager, that he (Stendahl) heard for the first time the light, spontaneous airs of Mozart, the sole composer he was to admit to his heart by the side of Cimarosa. The musician of the South and the one of the North satisfied his two dominant moods—gaiety and melancholy. "On the days of happiness, you unhesitatingly give your preference to Cimarosa," he wrote a few years later. "In the moments of dreamy and enchanting melancholy that you find at the end of autumn in the vicinity of an ancient castle under the long pathways of sycamores where the all-embracing silence is disturbed from time to time only by the rustle of the falling leaves, it is the genius of Mozart you love to come across. You wish to hear one of his airs played in the forest by a distant horn."

From a letter in the above volume to Pauline———, October 6, 1807:

Here are the principal works of Mozart, a musician born for his art, but a soul of the North, better fitted to depict unhappiness or the tranquility produced by its absence than the ecstasies and gracefulness that the mild climate of the South bestows upon its inhabitants. As a man of ideas and sensibility, he's infinitely to be preferred, the artists say, to all the mediocre Italian composers; but, as a rule, he's far beneath Cimarosa.

A diary entry, October 1809:

Haydn passed away here about a month ago; he

was the son of a simple peasant and elevated himself to immortal creation through a sensitive soul and studies which gave him the means of transmitting to others the sensations he experienced. A week after his death, all the musicians of the city gathered at the Scottish church to execute Mozart's *Requiem* in his honor. I was there, and in uniform, in the second row; the first taken up by the great man's family—three or four poor little women in black with mean faces. The *Requiem* appeared to me to be too noisy and didn't interest me; but I'm beginning to understand *Don Giovanni*, which they give in German nearly every week at the Widen theater.

A diary entry, June 21, 1813:

I've just borrowed a fine piano, which has been placed in little bedroom, and a Monsieur———, piano teacher, has played the music of Mozart for an hour. Several of the pieces gave me delightful pleasure, others bored me. Good executants are bad music priests; they spoil the music by, for instance, playing only the fragments of sonatas.

From "The Life of Rossini" by Stendahl, translated and annotated by Richard N. Coe:

Not that the Germans are an unemotional race—God forbid that I should perpetrate so gross an injustice towards the country which has given the world a Mozart!

Now that Rossini has taught us to expect such an amazing wealth of musical ideas, and Mozart has taught us to look for profundity, I am afraid that it may be rather late in the day to start listening to music in the manner of Gluck.

So let us return to Mozart, and to the *violence* of his music, which is a phrase that all Italians tend to use. Mozart appeared upon the musical horizon of Italy almost at the same moment as Rosinni, in 1812; but I am strangely afraid that *he* will still be known and loved when Rosinni's star has faded into dust. For Mozart was an originator in every field, in everything he touched; he is like nobody, and nobody is like him; whereas Rossini yet bears faint resemblances to Cimarosa, to Guglielmi and Haydn.

. . . in the technical, purely mechanical aspect of his art, Mozart can never be surpassed; and any composer who attempted to out-do him on this count would be like a painter who tried to out-do Titian in the effectiveness and realism of his coloring, or like a dramatist who tried to better Racine in the purity of his verse or in the delicacy and restraint of his expression.

Mozart is like a mistress who is always serious and often sad, but whose very sadness is a fascination, discovering ever deeper springs of love; such women either create no impression at all, in which case they are called prudes; or else, if they leave their mark but once only, the scar lies deep, and heart and soul are lost to them completely and forever.

Raphael, incidentally, had much of the unostentatious perfection and many of the profound spiritual qualities which characterize Mozart.

. . . . All Italians have a great regard for Mozart; yet they do not adore him as we do; for they admire his incomparable qualities as a writer of symphonic music rather than his gifts as a composer of opera. They never refer to him except as one of the greatest geniuses who ever lived; yet, even in *Don Giovanni*, they are liable to detect the typical weaknesses of the German school—that is to say, *not enough vocal melody*; plenty of melody for the clarinet and plenty for the bassoon, but nothing, or next to nothing, for that finest of all instruments (when it is not shouting its head off!), *the human voice*.

Thomas Love Peacock

(1785–1866) was a self-educated man of letters, worked in London for the East India Company and was from 1812 a close friend of Shelley. His best known works are the novels *Headlong Hall* (1816), *Nightmare Abbey* (1818) and *Maid Marion* (1822).

From his criticism, quoted in "Pleasures of Music" ed. by Jacques Barzun:

(At London) liberties are taken more or less with the works of all masters, from the greatest to the least. Mozart himself does not escape them. Interpolation indeed he does escape. The audiences of the King's Theatre are justly strict in this one point only, that they will not permit the sewing on of an extraneous purple shred to any of his great and sacred textures. But garbled and mutilated his works are abominably, to fit the Procrustean bed of an inadequate company, or to quadrate with the manager's notions of the bad taste of the public. A striking instance of this is in the invariable performances of *Il Don Giovanni* without its concluding sestetto. Don Juan's first introduction to a modern English audience was in a pantomime (at Drury Lane we believe), which ended with the infernal regions a shower of fire, and a dance of devils. Mozart's opera has, properly, no such conclusion.

Le Nozze di Figaro and *Il Flauto Magico* both require a better and more numerous company than is ever assembled in this country. If we have in the former an Almaviva, a Figaro, a Contessa, and a Susanna, it is the usual extent of our good fortune. We have seldom an endurable Cherubino; Marcellina is generally a non-entity; Barbarino always so; Bartolo, Basilio, and Antonio take their chance, which is seldom good for any of them, and never for all; and Don Curzio is for the most part abrogated.

Il Don Giovanni and *Le Nozze di Figaro* are both specimens of excellently written libretti, separating most effectively the action and passion from the ratiocination of the originals; but we have seen the latter especially performed in such a manner, that if we had known nothing of it but from the representation, we should have found it incomprehensible; and this sort of experiment on things which we know well should make us cautious of pronouncing summary judgment on things of which we know nothing but from the showing of the King's Theatre.

Carl Maria Von Weber

(1786–1826) is known primarily as the founder of the German romantic opera school by reason of his three masterpieces, *Der Freischutz* (1821), *Euryanthe* (1821) and *Oberon* (1826). He was born in Eutin, Oldenburg, and after musical apprenticeship (including lessons at Salzburg from Michael Haydn) went on to write concertos for piano and other instruments, but his interest was always in opera. He was appointed for life as musical director of German opera in Dresden. He died in London a few months after the premiere there of *Oberon*. Incidentally, Constanze Mozart was his distant cousin.

From "Enchanted Wanderer" by Lucy Poate Stebbins and Richard Poate Stebbins:

[(Written by Weber of Prague):] "I found a taste in music strangely conditioned by the older Italian opera and the period of Mozart. There was a vague and unquiet spirit not certain itself what it desired. By its nature Italian opera demands few artists, but these must be highly gifted; a sprinkling of bright gems regardless of their setting . . . all else is subordinate and unimportant. The German digs deeper. He must have a work of art where every element combines in the perfect whole."

In the earlier days the young couple (Carl and Caroline Von Weber) were too poor to furnish both establishments (two homes), and their belongings had to be carried to Hosterwitz in springtime and back to Dresden in the fall. The elegant, spindle-legged piano stood close to the living-room window where the bust of Mozart regarded it with gentle speculation . . .

The garlands (sent to Weber after the success of "Der Freischutz") went to Dresden, and Lina hung them above the drawing-room mirror. Weber set the laurel wreath on the bust of Mozart with the words, "That belongs to you!" Weber was very proud of these withering tributes, and showing them once to a visitor remarked, in a manner half-modest, half-ironical, *"Die hat mir alle 'Der Freischutz' eingebracht."**

*"Der Freischutz" brought me in all these.

GIOACCHINO ANTONIO ROSSINI

(1792–1868), a native of Pesaro, Italy, enrolled at age 15 in the Bologna Conservatory but soon left. At age 18 his first opera was produced in Venice. Shortly his genius in this genre saw a procession on the boards, *Tancredi* (1813) and *L'Italiana in Algieri* (1813), culminating with *The Barber of Seville* (1816), after which Rossini was generally regarded as the opera composer *par excellence*. He moved to Paris in 1824 where his last masterpiece, *William Tell*, appeared in 1829. For the rest of his life he wrote little serious music.

From "Richard Wagner's Visit to Rossini" by Edmond Michotte, translated by Herbert Weinstock:

Rossini: . . . the first time a performance of the *Eroica*. That music bowled me over. I had only one thought: to meet that great genius, to see him, even if only once. I sounded out Salieri on the subject, knowing that he was on good terms with Beethoven.
Wagner: Salieri, the composer of *Les Danaides*?
Rossini: Exactly. In Vienna, where he had lived for a long time, he had attracted a lot of attention as the result of the vogue of several of his operas that were given at the Italian Theatre; in fact, he told me that he sometimes saw Beethoven, but warned me that because of his (Beethoven's) distrustful and fantastic character, what I was asking for could not be arranged easily. Incidentally, Salieri had enjoyed equally good relations with Mozart. After the latter's death, it was sug-

gested—and even seriously charged—that out of professional jealously he had killed him by means of a slow poison.

Wagner: That rumor still was current in Vienna in my time.

Rossini: One day I amused myself by saying to Salieri as a joke: 'It's a lucky thing for Beethoven that, out of an instinct for self-preservation, he avoids having you at meals; for you might well send him wandering in the other world, as you did Mozart.' 'Do I have the air of a poisoner, then?' Salieri asked. 'O no!' I answered, 'you have more the air of a real craven! ('l'air d'un fieffe c . . . ouard!)—which, in fact, he was. That poor devil, what is more, seemed to have little taste for passing as Mozart's assassin . . .

Rossini: . . . .Ah! I feel that if I had been able to take my scholastic studies in your (Wagner's) country I should have been able to produce something better than what is known of mine!

Wagner: Surely not better—to cite only the Scene des tenebris in your *Moise*, the conspiracy in Guillaume Tell, or, of another sort, the Quando Corpus morietur . . .

Rossini: I'll have to concede that you have mentioned some happy episodes of my career. But what is all that alongside the work of Mozart, of a Haydn? I don't know how to tell you strongly enough how much I admire those masters for that supple science, that certainty which is so natural to them in the art of composing. I have always envied them that; but it must be learned on the school benches, and one most also be a Mozart to know how to profit by it . . .

Wagner: . . . Don't they (the public) represent me as an arrogant man . . . denigrating Mozart?
Rossini: (with a touch of humor): Mozart, l'angelo della musica. . . . But who, short of sacrilege, would dare to touch him?

JOHN KEATS

(1795–1821), best known for his lyric poetry, is considered one of the greatest to write in English and whose name is commonly associated with those of Shelley and Byron, his contemporaries. Dying young, his mastery of images and sensuous language was so monumental that many believe death robbed literature of its greatest lyricist.

From "Complete Works of John Keats" edited by H. B. Forman:

Letter of October 1818 to George and Georgiana Keats referring to an unnamed woman: "She kept me awake one night, as a tune of Mozart's might do."

Franz Peter Schubert

(1797–1828) was born in Vienna and although now recognized as one of the supreme melodists, was virtually unappreciated in his lifetime except by a coterie of friends on whom he depended even for creature support. Prolific, in his short life he composed hundreds of songs, nine symphonies, string quartets, masses and operettas.

From "Schubert - Memories by His Friends" ed. and collected by Otto Erich Deutsch:

Reported by Josef Von Spaun: . . . of the G Minor Symphony by Mozart he (Schubert) often said to me that it produced in him a violent emotion without his knowing exactly why. He declared the Minuet in this symphony to be enchanting and in the Trio it seemed to him that the angels were singing too. . . . After a successful performance of the Overture to *Nozze di Figaro* he cried out, full of enthusiasm, "that is the most beautiful overture in the whole world" but then added after some reflection "I had almost forgotten *Die Zauberflote*."

I once found him alone in the music-room sitting at the piano which, with his little hands, he already played quite nicely. He was just trying through a Mozart sonata and said that he liked it very much but that he found Mozart very difficult to play well.

Schubert is represented as having an extraordinary admiration for Beethoven; now this is quite true, as he had a whole-hearted enthusiasm for the creations of this great master; but his admiration for

Mozart was just as great, and unattainable as Beethoven's symphonies seemed to him to be, he nevertheless far preferred "Don Juan" to "Fidelio," much as he liked the latter too, and the overture to "Die Zauberflote" held a higher place in his esteem than the beautiful overtures to "Fidelio." Mozart's *Requiem* he declared to be divine, unattainable work.

Reported by Karl von Braunthal: Schubert said: "He (Beethoven) can do everything but we cannot understand everything yet, and much water will flow under the Danube bridge before what this man has written becomes generally understood. It is not only that he is the most sublime and the most prolific of all composers, he is also the most daring; he is as much master of dramatic as he is of epic music, of the music of poetry as of the music of prose; in a word, he can do everything. Mozart is to him as Schiller is to Shakespeare; Schiller is already understood, Shakespeare not by a long way. Everyone understands Mozart, no one really understands Beethoven, for such a person would need to have great intellect and still more depth of feeling and to have been desperately unhappy in love or to have been unhappy in some other way.

Reported by Gerhard Von Breuning: ... shortly after Schubert had been introduced to us and was coming to the musical evenings which I used to give at that time at our house; we had just sung the trios and other things from *Die Zauberflote* and he said over and over again—Bless my soul! I can see him still, folding his hands together as if in prayer, because he was so moved, and pressing them against his mouth, as he used to do when he heard something beautiful—'Heavens! How beautiful that is . . .'

Reported by Anselm Huttenbrenner: Schubert's. . . . favorite compositions were:
> Handel's oratorio, "Messiah."
> Mozart's "Don Giovanni" and "Requiem."
> Beethoven's "Adelaide," C major Mass
> and C minor Symphony.

Schubert was enormously captivated by Mozart's operas, especially by "Don Giovanni," "Zauberflote," "Figaro" and the ensemble pieces (numbers) in "Idomeneo." Mozart was, for him, the finest model for opera composers.

Quote from Schubert's diary, dated Vienna, 14 June 1816, from "The Schubert Reader" by Otto Erich Deutsch:

A light, bright, fine day this will remain throughout my whole life. As from afar the magic notes of Mozart's music still gently haunt me. How unbelievably vigorously, and yet again how gently, was it impressed deep, deep into the heart by Schlesinger's masterly playing. Thus does our soul retain these fair impressions, which no time, no circumstances can efface, and they lighten our existence. They show us in the darkness of this life a bright, clear lovely distance, for which we hope with confidence. O Mozart, immortal Mozart, how many, oh how endlessly many such comforting perceptions of a brighter and better life hast thou brought to our souls!

VIVA MOZART

Quote from a letter Schubert wrote to his brother Ferdinand dated 21 September 1825 regarding a journey:

A few hours later we reached the curious but extremely dirty and horrid town of Hallein. The inhabitants all look like ghosts, pale, hollow-eyed and lean enough to catch fire. The appalling contrast of the sight of such a rat-hole, etc., in this valley made the most dismal impression on me. It was as though one had fallen from heaven into a dung-heap or were listening after Mozart's music to a piece by the immortal A.

GAETANO DONIZETTI

(1797–1848), one of Italy's 'great five:' (Rossini, Bellini, Verdi, Puccini), was born in Bergamo and scheduled at first for the law but entered the music school at Bologna where he devoted his talent to opera so prolifically that there are seventy-five with his name on them. Many are among opera's greatest treasures: *L'elisir d'amore* (1832), *Lucia di Lammermoor* (1835), *Roberto Devereux* (1837), *La Fille du regiment* (1840), *La Favorita* (1840), *Linda di Chamonix* (1842) and *Don Pasquale* (1843) to name only a few.

From "Donizetti" by William Ashbrook:

On July 3, 1842 the appointment (Hofkapellmeister to the Emperor of Austria) was formally made with a salary of 12,000 lire a year, and accepted. Donizetti found great satisfaction in this honor, which seemed to insure him a place in history.

(Later Donizetti wrote to Toto, his brother-in-law):
... Your blame for my accepting the most honorable post is unjust. Six months free are a fine thing; a thousand lire a month at Vienna and away are not to be despised. Do you know that at Bologna they only wanted to grant three months' leave at a time? Do you know that I would have to be without fail in Bologna on S. Petronio's Day? That it would not be enough to compose new music, I would be wanted there in person?.... Do you know, on the other hand, that my post was Mozart's? ...

EUGENE DELACROIX

(1798–1863) was born into a wealthy French family and at age 17 entered the studio of the painter Guerin, exhibiting his own allegoric paintings at the Paris Salon in 1822. His paintings had great influence on the Impressionists Renoir and Manet though he himself was of the older Romantic school.

From the Journal (1853–1856), quoted in "Pleasures of Music" ed. by Jacques Barzun:

I dined at Princess Marcelline's: duets for piano and bass by Mozart and Beethoven ... What a life mine is! I was thinking of this while listening to this superb music, especially Mozart's, which suggests the calm of an orderly epoch. I have come to the time of life when the tumult of passion no longer intrudes upon the delightful emotions aroused by objects of beauty. I have no knowledge of the paper work and drudgery that form the occupation of most men. Instead of thinking about business, I think only of Rubens or Mozart; my chief concern for a week at a time is a melody or a picture . . .

Mozart is modern . . . that is, he is not afraid to touch on the melancholy side of things, but, like the men of his time—French gaiety, the being compelled to deal only with attractive things and to banish from art and conversation whatever is gloomy and serves to recall our human condition—Mozart combines just enough of this touch of pleasurable sadness with the easy cheerfulness and elegance of a mind lucky enough to take in what is agreeable.

. . . How different is Chopin! Just see . . . how much he is a man of his own time, how he makes use of the advances that others have contributed to his art, how he loves Mozart with out being like him.

Hector Berlioz

(1803–1869) was born in Cote-Saint-Andre, France. He briefly studied medicine in Paris but in 1825 was enrolled at the Paris Conservatory and in 1830 introduced his masterpiece, the *Symphonie Fantastique*, inspired by his (at the time) unrequited love for an English actress, Harriet Simpson whom he later married. Meanwhile he produced a series of great orchestral and operatic works: *Harold in Italy* (1834), *Romeo and Juliet* (1839), *The Damnation of Faust* (1846) and the heroic opera *Les Troyens* (1853). He also wrote a great deal of music criticism, and his *Memoirs* (1870) is a landmark in literature of its kind.

From a letter quoted by Humphrey Searle in "Hector Berlioz" dated May 1856:

Offenbach has invented (rearranged) an opera by Mozart, the *Impressario*, of which all the Press are singing praises. I haven't seen it and am glad, for if I had I would probably find it ridiculous, and I adore Mozart.

From "Memoirs of Hector Berlioz":

. . . in order to ensure the success of Mozart's *Magic Flute*, the manager of the (Paris) Opera produced that marvellous travesty of it, *Les Mysteres d'Isis*, the libretto of which is a mystery as yet unveiled by no one. When he had manipulated the text of this masterpiece to his liking, our intelligent manager sent for a *German* composer to help him patch up the music. The German proved equal to the occasion. He stuck a few bars on to the end of the overture (the overture to the *Magic Flute!*), turned the soprano part of a chorus (*Per voi risplendi il giorno*) into a bass aria, adding a few bars of his own; transplanted the wind instruments from one scene to another; changed the air and altered the instrumental accompaniment in Sarastro's glorious aira; manufactured a song out of the slaves' chorus, *O cara armonia*; and converted a duet into a trio. Not satisfied with the *Magic Flute*, this harpy must next glut himself on *Titus* and *Don Giovanni*. The aria *Quel charme a mes esprits rappelle* is taken from *Titus*, but only the *andante* is there, for the *allegro*, with which it ends, does not seem to have pleased our *uomo capace*; so he decreed a violent divorce, and, in its stead, put in a patchwork of his own, interspersed with scraps of Mozart. No one would dream of the base uses to which our friend put the celebrated *Fin ch' han dal vino*, that vivid outburst of libertinism in which Don Giovanni's whole character is epitomized. He turned it into a trio for a bass and two sopranos, with the following sweetly sentimental lines:

> Heureux delire!
>   Mon coeur soupire!
> Que mon sort differe du sien!
> Quel plaisir est egal au mien!
>   Crois ton amie,
>   C'est pour la vie
> Que mon sort va s'unir au tien.
>   O douce ivresse
>   De la tendresse!
> Ma main te presse,
> Dieu! quel grand bien!

When this wretched hotch-potch was ready it was dubbed The Mysteries of Isis, was played in that form, and printed and published in full score with the name of that profound idiot Lachnith (which I publish that it may be perpetuated with that of Castilblaze) actually bracketed with Mozart's on the title-page.

In this wise, and at twenty years' interval, two beggars in filthy rags came masquerading before the public in the rich robes of the kings of harmony; and in this sordid fashion two men of genius, disguised as monkeys, decked in flimsy tinsel, blinded, mutilated and deformed, were presented to the French people, by their tormentors, as Mozart and Weber!

And the public was deceived, for no one came forward to punish the miscreants or give them the lie.

I have stated that when I went up for my first examination at the Conservatoire, I was wholly absorbed in the study of dramatic music of the grand school; I should have said of lyrical tragedy, and it was owing to this cause that my admiration of Mozart was so lukewarm. Only Gluck and Spontini could excite me. And this was the reason for my coolness with regard to the composer of *Don Giovanni*. *Don Giovanni* and *Figaro* were the two of Mozart's works oftenest played in Paris; but they were always given in Italian, by Italians, at the Italian Opera; and that alone was sufficient to prejudice me against them. Their great defect in my eyes was that they seemed to belong to the ultramontane school. Another and more legitimate objection was a passage in the part of Donna Anna which shocked me greatly, where Mozart has inserted a wretched vocalise which is a perfect blot on his brilliant work. It occurs in the allegro of the soprano aria in the second act, *Non mir dir*, a song of intense sadness, in which all the poetry of love finds vent in lamentation and tears, and which is yet made to wind up with such a ridiculous, unseemly phrase that one wonders how the same man could have written both. Donna Anna seems suddenly to have dried her tears and broken out into coarse buffoonery. The words of this passage are, *Forse un giorno il cielo ancora sentira-a-a-* (here comes an incredible run, in execrable taste) *pieta di me*. A truly singular form of expression for a noble, outraged woman, of the *hope that heaven will one day have pity on her!* ... I found it difficult to forgive Mozart for this enormity. Now I feel that I would shed my blood if I could thereby erase that shameful page and others of the same kind which disfigure some of his work.[1]

I therefore received his dramatic doctrines with distrust, and my enthusiasm fell to just one degree above freezing point. Still I felt the warmest admiration for the religious grandeur of the *Magic Flute*; though I had only heard it in its travestied form as *The Mysteries of Isis*, and it was not until afterwards that I was able to compare the original score in the Conservatoire library with the wretched French *pot-pourri* played at the Opera.

As I first heard the works of this great composer under such disadvantageous circumstances, it was only many years later that I was able to appreciate their charm and suave perfection. The wonderful beauty of his quartets and quintets, and some of his sonatas, first converted me to the worship of this angelic genius, whose brightness was slightly dimmed by intercourse with Italians and contrapuntal pedagogues.

---

[1] Even the epithet "shameful" scarcely seems to me strong enough to blast this passage. Mozart has there committed one of the most flagrant crimes recorded in history of art against passion, feeling, good taste, and good sense. (B.)

A learned abbe, belonging to the Sistine Chapel, told Mendelssohn *that he had heard someone speak of a young man of great promise called Mozart*. It is true that this worthy ecclesiastic does not often come into contact with the world, and has studied nothing but Palestrina all his life. So he may be regarded as an exceptional being, for though Mozart's music is never played in Rome, still a good many people there have heard something more of him than that he was a *young man of great promise*. The more learned amateurs even know that he is dead, and that though he cannot be classed with Donizetti, he has written some remarkable works. I knew one who had a copy of *Don Giovanni*; and after studying it for some time on the piano, he confided to me that he thought *this old music* was really better then the *Zadig* or *Astartea* of M. Vaccai, which has just been brought out at the Apollo Theatre. Instrumental music is a sealed book to the Romans. They have not the most elementary notion of what we call a symphony.

The Stuttgart orchestra is composed of 16 violins, 4 violas, 4 cellos, 4 basses, and the wind and percussion instruments necessary to perform most of the modern operas; there is also an excellent harpist, one Kruger, and this is rare for Germany. The study of that fine instrument is neglected here, for no discoverable reason, in an absurd and even barbarous way. Indeed I am inclined to believe that this was always the case, considering that none of the German masters have ever made use of it. There is no harp part in any of Mozart's works,[1] neither in *Don Giovanni*, *Figaro*, the *Magic Flute*, the *Seraglio*, *Idomeneo*, *Cosi fan tutte*, nor in his masses or symphonies. Weber also abstained from using it, likewide Haydn and Beethoven. Gluck alone wrote an easy harp part in *Orfeo, for one hand only*, and anyhow that opera was composed and represented in Italy. There is something in this at once amazing and annoying to me.

. . . .My desire to visit Prague became as great as the fear I formerly had of showing myself there. When the Viennese heard that I had made up my mind to go, they did not spare their witticisms at my expense. "The inhabitants of Prague claim to have discovered Mozart; they swear by him, care for no symphonies but his. They will give it to you finely," etc. But . . . I set off notwithstanding the gloomy forebodings of the mockers.

From "Mozart, Weber & Wagner" by Hector Berlioz:

Generally speaking, the melody of this opera ("Il Seraglio") is simple, sweet and not very original; being provided with accompaniments which are discreet, agreeable, but slightly varied, and childish. The instrumentation is simply that of the period; but already better disposed than in the works of the author's contemporaries. The score contains fre-

---

[1] Berlioz omits to mention the Harp Concerti; he may not have been acquainted with the whole range of Mozart's output.

quent instances of what then went by the name of "Turkish music;" consisting of bass-drum, cymbals and triangle, employed in an altogether primitive manner. Besides that, Mozart has used a small 'fifth' flute in G (called 'in A,' at the period when ordinary flutes were considered as being in D); and he sometimes formed a trio by using this G instrument with the two large flutes.

If the first air of Osmin bore the name of any living composer, we should be justified in finding it altogether deprived of interest; and, if the three verses, afterwards sung by the same character, had been regarded in this way, they certainly would not have had to be repeated. . . .

"Il Seraglio," according to all our critical colleages, was treated at the (Paris) Theatre-Lyrique with *scrupulous fidelity*. This means that all they did was:

1. To invert the order of succession of several numbers.

2. To take out a grand air from the part of Madame Meillet, and insert it into that of Madame Ugalde;

3. To play, between their *two* acts the famous Turkish march, so well known to pianists; and—

4. To render in *two* acts what had been written for *three*. Well! well! not so bad for what they call a *scrupulous fidelity*.

Mikhail Ivanovich Glinka

(1804–1857), often called the Father of Russian music, was born in Smolensk of a wealthy family and received little formal musical training though studying piano and composing as a young man. After further study in St. Petersburg, he wrote his opera *A Life for the Czar* (1836) that reflected his national style. With *Russlan and Ludmilla* (1842) he became the quintessential Russian operatic genius whose work in that genre has eclipsed his many compositions for orchestra, piano and voice.

From "Mikhail Ivanovich Glinka - Memoirs" translated by Richard B. Mudge, Univ. of Oklahoma Press, Norman, 1963:

In 1843 Ulybyshev sent me his book on Mozart. I read part of it and studied anew all Mozart's operas from the scores. The remarks and criticism of Count M. Yu. Vielegorsky and this work I did on Mozart stimulated my critical spirit, which was further excited a little later on.

In the winter . . . we had some Italian theatre . . . Among other things, they put on Mozart's *Don Juan*. All the principal roles were murdered; only Zerlina (Viardot) and Masetto (Artemovsky) were played well.

Felix Mendelssohn

(1809–1847), born in Hamburg, Germany, to a wealthy family, as early as 1826 became famous as the composer of *A Midsum-*

mer *Night's Dream Overture* and went on to become one of the most popular conductors and composers of his day. His vogue was great not only in Germany where he received many honors and helped found the Leipzig Conservatory but he was especially popular in England, there introducing such familar works as *Fingal's Cave Overture*, the *G Minor Piano Concerto* and his *Songs Without Words* (1833). His five symphonies are regularly found in repertories today, and the *E Minor Violin Concerto* is a standard showpiece for that instrument.

From "Letters" edited by G. Seldon Goth:

"It always makes me furious when men who have no pursuit presume to judge others who wish to achieve something, however small. I therefore took the liberty recently of rebuking a certain musician in society here. He began to speak of Mozart, and as Bunsen and his sister love Palestrina, he tried to flatter their tastes by asking me, for instance, what I thought of the worthy Mozart, and all his sins. I replied, however, that as far as I was concerned, I should be only too happy to renounce all my virtues in exchange for Mozart's sins; but that of course I could not venture to determine the extent of his virtues. The people all laughed, and were much amused. To think that such a person should have no awe of so great a name!

. . . I am very weary and exhausted from yesterday's concert, where, in addition to conducting three times, I was obliged to play Mozart's D minor concerto. In the first movement I made a cadenza which succeeded wonderfully and caused a tremendous sensation among the Leipzigers. I must write down the end for you. You remember the theme, of course. Towards the close of the cadence, arpeggios come in pianissimo in D minor thus . . . Our second violin player, an old musician, said to me afterwards, when he met me in the passage, that he had heard it played in the same hall by Mozart himself, but since that day he had heard no one introduce such good cadenzas as I did yesterday—which gave me very great pleasure.

Edward FitzGerald

(1809–1883) was born near Woodbridge, Suffolk, and educated at Cambridge. A prolific letter writer and amateur musician, he is best known for his translation of the *Rubaiyat of Omar Khayyam* (1859).

From "With Friends Possessed - a Life of Edward FitzGerald" by Robert Gernard Martin:

He (FitzGerald) told Frederick Tennyson: 'Mozart, I agree with you, is the most universal musical genius; Beethoven has been too analytical and erudite . . .'

In thanking Fanny Kemble for a paper she had written about the stage, he said, 'I always think that your Theory of the Intuitive versus the Analytical and Philosophical applies to other Arts as well as that of the Drama. Mozart couldn't tell how he made a

Tune; even a whole Symphony, he said, unrolled itself out of a leading idea by no logical process. Keats said that no Poetry was worth (anything) unless it came spontaneously, as Leaves to a Tree, etc. I have no faith in your Works of Art done on Theory and Principle, like Wordsworth, Wagner, Holman Hunt, etc.'

FREDERIC CHOPIN

(1810–1849) was born in Warsaw, Poland, a musical prodigy who gave a first piano concert at age 7 and in his short life became the most famous composer of music for the piano. He spent most of his life in Paris, was involved romantically with the French novelist, George Sand, whose influence on him was destructive; nevertheless he produced much of his best work during the years with her, the largest of which are his two *Piano Concertos*, No. 1 (1830), No. 2 (1829). He died in poverty of tuberculosis.

From "Chopin, the Man and His Music" by Herbert Weinstock:

. . . Important for Chopin's reputation among his friends and contemporaries was his Opus 2, also composed or completed during his eighteenth year. "*La ci darem la mano*, varied for piano with orchestra accompaniment," dedicated to his most adored friend Tytus Woyiechowski would be published in Vienna in 1830. Then it would win for its creator a ringing salute from the slightly younger paladin of musical romanticism, Robert Schumann. It was to make Chopin's a familiar name in the German states.

Today it is all but forgotten. Between the extreme of Schumann's overpraise and today's neglect lies the fate the piece's inherent qualities justify. The music has, in addition to the irrepressible beauty of Mozart's duet, a plethora of surface charms. What it altogether lacks is original musical ideas.

From "The Life and Death of Chopin" by Casimir Wierzynski:

In a letter to his mistress, Delphine Potocka: There are few geniuses capable of understanding all instruments and bringing out all the potentialities of each one. I know of only two such men—Bach and Mozart. Even Beethoven is not so universal in scope . . .

In another letter to her: Mozart encompasses the entire domain of musical creation, but I've got only the keyboard in my poor head. I know my limitations, and I know that I'd make a fool of myself if I tried to climb too high without having the ability to do it. They plague me to death urging me to write symphonies and operas, and they want me to be everything in one, a Polish Rossini and a Mozart and a Beethoven. But I just laugh under my breath and think to myself that one must start from small things. I'm only a pianist . . .

Robert Schumann

(1810–1856) was born in Zwikau, Germany, and began the study of law at Leipzig University but at about age 20 began taking instruction under Freidrich Wieck as a pianist. This endeavor was aborted when he injured a finger, so he began composing and writing musical criticism. (Chopin was one of his 'discoveries.') He married Wieck's daughter Clara, herself a concert pianist who performed many of her husband's works, especially the *Piano Concerto in A Minor* (1845) and his many piano pieces. His symphonies are standard concert fare, and his songs are often sung. After gradually losing his mind, he died in an asylum at Endenich.

From "The Musical World of Robert Schumann" by Henry Pleasants:

It is ever with a sense of awe that I have approached the works of Mozart, whose influence was so great and extensive. Should this clear way of thinking and poetizing give way to something more formless and mystical, as suggested by the forces whose shadows now encroach upon all the arts, let us not forget the beautiful epoch which Mozart dominated and which Beethoven then shook until it shuddered at every joint, conceivably not entirely without his Prince Wolfgang's sanction.

Ah, Mozart, Prince of Spirits in that other world founded by the most beautiful of human faiths, call together one day—and may it be a long time off— all those disciples who, in this world, have borne the German name of Ludwig! (referring to musicians, of course headed by Beethoven)

Mozart, an elfin spirit, on bright moonlit nights gathered the dew-soaked buds of his art in magic groves . . .

(Referring to a certain piece of "program music"

by Louis Sphor) We confess to a bias against this sort of creation and share it, perhaps, with hundreds of learned men, many of whom have singular ideas about the process of composition and never fail to cite Mozart as an example of one who composed without thinking of anything in particular. If a composer shows me his composition along with such a programme I say: 'First show me that you can make beautiful music; after that I may well like your programme.'

From Schumann's journalism, quoted in "Pleasures of Music" ed. by Jacques Barzun:

Beethoven looks different on paper from Mozart, something like the difference between Jean-Paul's prose style and Goethe's. Here in this new work (Chopin's *"Variations on La Ci Darem La Mano"*) it seemed as if strange eyes were staring wonderingly at me—flowerlike eyes, eyes of baselisks, of peacocks, of maidens. In places the pattern grew clearer; I thought I discerned Mozart's *"La ci darem la mano"* intertwined with a hundred chords. Leporello seemed to wink at me as Don Juan flew past in his white cloak . . .

. . ."I should say that is certainly something—Chopin! I've never heard the name.—Who can he be?—A genius anyhow! . . ."

Otto Nicolai

(1810–1849) was born in Konigsberg, Germany, and in 1827 moved to Berlin, making his concert debut there as composer, vocalist and pianist in 1833. Among his many accomplishments as a musician is his having conducted the inaugural concert of the Vienna Philharmonic Orchestra in 1842, an event that has been commemorated annually in his name for many years. He lived only two months after the first production of his masterpiece, *The Merry Wives of Windsor* (1849).

From a review of Nicolai's "Merry Wives of Windsor" by Andrew Porter:

Otto Nicolai's "Merry Wives of Windsor" (1849) is a delightful opera, one in which 'wit, merry humors, the wildest jesting, craft, and daring'—as evoked by Mistress Ford at the start of her aria—conspire with charm, in music well enough composed to beguile the nicest ear. Mozart, Weber, Donizetti, and Mendelssohn were Nicolai's musical godparents, and what they bestowed on him he used well. He hesitated to take on a "Falstaff" opera—only a Mozart, he declared, was fit companion for a Shakespeare—but when he did so he produced a work that even Verdi's masterpiece on the same subject (1893) has not extinguished.

William Makepeace Thackeray

(1811–1863) was born in Calcutta, son of an Englishman working for the East India Company but came to England at age 6.

VIVA MOZART

After haphazard schooling he at last entered Cambridge but did not graduate. Starting as a journalist in London he soon published the novels *Barry Lyndon* (1844) and his masterpiece *Vanity Fair* (1847). His other major novels are *Pendennis* and *Henry Esmond*.

From "Vanity Fair" (1847):

Chapter XLIX

She (Becky Sharp) sang religious songs of Mozart, which had been early favorites of Lady Steyne, and with such sweetness and tenderness that the lady lingering around the piano, sat down by its side, and listened until the tears rolled down her eyes.

Chapter LXII

Here it was that Emmy (Amelia) found her delight and was introduced for the first time to the wonders of Mozart (and Cimarosa). The major's (Dobbin's) musical taste has been before alluded to and his performance on the flute commended. But perhaps the chief pleasure he had in these operas was in watching Emmy's rapture while listening to them. A new world of love and beauty broke upon her when she was introduced to those divine compositions; this lady had the keenest and finest sensibility, and how could she be indifferent when she heard Mozart? The tender parts of Don Juan awakened in her raptures so exquisite that she would ask herself when she went to say her prayers at night whether it was not wicked to feel so much delight as that with which "Vedrai Carino" and "Batti Batti" filled her gentle little bosom?

From "Pendennis" (1850):

Chapter XVIII

The next night he (Pendennis) came in late, and stayed very quietly for the after-piece, and on the third and last night of his stay in London—why, Taglioni was going to dance at the Opera—Taglioni! and there was to be *Don Giovanni*, which he admired of all things in the world: so Mr. Pen went to *Don Giovanni* and Taglioni.

Chapter XLV

Colchicum was in attendance upon Mademoiselle Caracoline, little Tom Tufthunt was in attendance upon Lord Colchicum; and rather pleased, too, with his position. When Don Juan scales the wall, there's never a want of a Leporello to hold the ladder.

From "Notes of a Journey from Cornhill to Grand Cairo" London, 1846:

After you have seen it (The Ruins of Telmessus), the remembrance of it remains with you, like a tune from Mozart which he seems to have caught out of Heaven, and which rings sweet harmony in your ears for ever after. It's a benefit for all after life!

From "Sketches and Travel in London" London, 1879:

When she comes into the room, it is like a beautiful air of Mozart breaking upon you.

Franz Liszt

(1811–1886), a native of Hungary, first became a European sensation as a pianist after an 1824 debut in Paris. Not only a flamboyant performer, he composed orchestral and piano works that are still in the concert repertory, including *Les Preludes* (1854), several *Hungarian Rhapsodies* (1846–1885) and the popular *Liebestraum* (1850). His personal life was turbulent with love affairs; one of his daughters, Cosima, left her husband to marry Richard Wagner.

Quoting De Beaufort in his Life of Liszt, *in* Ferencz Liszt *by Frederick Corder, Harper & Bros., New York, 1925):*

Franz's success was such that he could never hope there after to surpass it. . . . The press indulged in extravagant praise, pointing to Franz as 'the eighth wonder of the world;' people put him in a parallel with Mozart and affected to say that his talent for the piano was superior to that of Moscheles.

From "The Letters of Franz Liszt" translated and edited by Howard E. Hugo:

December 10, 1872
. . . Schubert's very successful statue in the *Stadt-Park* doesn't seem to me to be a definite obstacle against the quintuple-monument: the chief difficulty rests in the composition of the group. To my way of thinking the place in the center belongs to Mozart, due to the universality of his genius; but how should the others be grouped and shown?. . .

―――1875

Mozart and Goethe had as their first name: *Wolfgang*. May Mozart's charming melodies and Goethe's Olympian serenity haunt your *Ocean Villa* at Wolfgang!

Richard Wagner

(1813–1883) was born in Leipzig and by many is regarded as Germany's greatest composer of opera, though he began writing operas that utterly failed. He was usually insolvent and once was jailed for debts; nevertheless he persevered, and after the production of *Rienzi* (1842) and *The Flying Dutchman* (1843) became director of the Dresden Opera and produced *Tannhauser* and *Lohengrin* (1850). Before his death in Venice he had given the world *Tristan and Isolde* (1865), *The Mastersingers* (1868), *The Rhinegold* (1869), *The Valkyries* (1870) and *Parsifal* (1882). A complex and difficult man, his genius lay not in human relationships but in pure music.

From "Wagner: Stories and Essays" edited by Charles Osborn quoting Wagner:

"The language of Bach stands in the same relationship to that of Mozart, and finally Beethoven, as the Egyptian Sphinx does to Greek figure sculpture: as the human face of the Sphinx strives to escape from the animal body, so the noble human features of Bach strive to dissociate themselves from the powdered wig . . .

"Even the urge toward powerfulness can become

a curse for us (Germans), by betraying us into a fantastic self-complacency. That Goethe and Schiller, Mozart and Beethoven have issued from the German nation, far too easily tempts the mass of middling talents to consider these great minds similar to themselves by right of birth, and persuades them into imagining themselves Goethes and Schillers, Mozarts and Beethovens. Nothing is more conducive to sloth and laziness than a high opinion of oneself, the idea that one is something intrinsically great and need take no pains to improve oneself.

"Beethoven immensely enlarged the form of the symphony when he discarded the proportions of the older musical period which had attained their utmost beauty in Mozart, and followed his impatient genius with bolder but ever more conclusive freedom to regions where he alone could venture. As he also knew how to give those soaring flights a philosophical coherence, it is undeniable that upon the basis of the Mozart symphony he reared a wholly new artistic genre, which he at the same time perfected in every point. But Beethoven would not have been able to achieve all this, had Mozart not previously addressed his conquering genius to the symphony also; had his animating, idealising breath not given a spiritual warmth to the soulless forms and diagrams accepted up till then. It is from this point that Beethoven departed and the artist who had taken Mozart's divinely pure soul unto himself could never descend from that high altitude which is true music's domain.

From Cosima Wagner's Diaries, Vol 1:

He (Wagner) says that up to Mozart music remained in a vegetable state, but with Mozart and particularly with Beethoven "anima" had entered into it. The Bachian fugue was like a great tree, so lofty and also imposing, yet in a completely different way from the human heart.

In the evening R. (Wagner) and Richter play Mozart's C Major Symphony as a piano duet, in the course of which R. gets very indignant about the faulty arrangement: "That is just like the Germans —always carrying on about Mozart, and then they produce such editions!"

He (Wagner) comes back to Mozart and says he wants to build the whole philosophy of music out of one movement of a Mozart symphony; precisely because it is so simple and melodically so infinitely free.

Afternoon with R. (Wagner), played the *Faust* Overture and two Haydn symphonies, during which he remarked that in matters of form Haydn is a greater master than Mozart.

Conversations at supper bring us to Mozart. Dealing with *Die Zauberflöte*, R. says, "Mozart is the founder of German declamation—what fine humanity resounds in the Priest's replies to Tamino! Think how stiff such high priests are in Gluck. When you consider this text, which was meant to be a farce,

VIVA MOZART

and the theatre for which it was written, and compare what was written before Mozart's time (even Cimarosa's still-famous *Matrimonio Segreto*)—on the one side the wretched German *Singspiel*, on the other the ornate Italian opera—one is amazed by the soul he managed to breathe into such a text. And what a life he led! A bit of tinsel at the time of his popularity, but for that he then had to pay all the more dearly. He did not complete his work, which is why one cannot really compare him with Raphael, for there is still too much convention in him.

Then R. plays us passages from *Entfuhrung* and *Figaro*—he likes the old Simrock editions. When Prof. N. remarks that Mozart is said to have invented the music of intrigue, R. replies that, on the contrary, he resolved intrigue into melody. One has only to compare Beaumarchais's (incidentally excellent) play with Mozart's opera to see that the former contains cunning, clever and calculating people who deal and talk wittily with one another, while in Mozart they are transfigured, suffering, sorrowing human beings.

Richter recently said of Mozart that it was just as well he died, otherwise he would have fallen into mannerisms, or his ingratiating melodies would forever have made people incapable of grasping the art of Beethoven. R. reproached him earnestly for this, pointing out that Mozart had only just reached mastery when he died, and we could never know what treasures he might have given us. "One must not take the easy way and say that everyone dies at the proper time. What would I not give for Beethoven's tenth symphony! Even if I, too, believe that everyone as a general rule is given the chance to show what he is made of, a truly great genius always dies too soon; it is not as with Mendelssohn, Schubert, Schumann, minds of the second, third or fourth rank."

(Wagner said): "I recently read that Hanslick had spoken of Beethoven's naivete. A donkey like that can of course have no idea of the wisdom of genius, which, though it comes and goes like lightning, is the highest there is. One could rather call Mozart naive, because he worked in forms he did not create himself—only what he said within them was his own. The wisdom of genius is of course entirely spontaneous, not considered."

R. says, "A Bach fugue is like a crystal forming, then solidifying on the pedal point." Then he said of Beethoven and Mozart, "As far as fugues are concerned, these gentlemen can hide their heads before Bach, they played with the form, wanted to show they could do it, too, but he showed us the soul of the fugue, he could not do otherwise than write in fugues."

We talked a lot about the 9th Symphony, which is so awkward in many technical details, yet throughout so intoxicating in the power of its thought. "It is true 'tragelaph,' " R. says, laughing. He feels it would be very much to the advantage of the work if much of it were to be reorchestrated. "In regard to form Mozart seems a true Alexandrian master compared with Beethoven."

Cosima's own entry:

It seems as if Life and Death have no real power over mortals such as Weber, Beethoven and Mozart; it is as if they were of all time and had been with us only as the spirits they are now. With less gifted human beings life is everything, and they can only be forgotten, they cannot dominate the realm of shadows. As long as mortals who once knew them continue to live, their earthly presence remains fresh, whereas their spiritual essence fades, one remembers and talks of them without awe; in the case of true genius it is the other way around—the spirit becomes ever more alive, while the form in which it was clothed eventually takes on the appearance of a shadow.

From "Opera and Drama" by Richard Wagner, 1851:

Did the critic imagine he could make this proof (that Mendelssohn could write an opera) dependent on the peculiarly gifted musical personality? Was Mozart a lesser musician? Is it possible to find anything more perfect than every piece of his *Don Juan*?

VIVA MOZART

"*Good heavens, young man, I didn't know Mozart could come out of one of those things.*"

Drawing by W. Miller; © 1983 The New Yorker Magazine, Inc.

From "Prose Works II" by Richard Wagner. Translated by William Ashton Ellis:

The noble, straightforward simplicity of his (Mozart's) purely musical instinct, for instance his instinctive penetration into the arcana of his art, made it well-nigh impossible to him *there* to bring forth magical effects, as Composer, where the Poem was flat and meaningless. How little did this richest-gifted of all musicians understand our modern music-makers' trick of building gaudy towers of music upon hollow, valueless foundation, and playing the rapt and the inspired where all the poetaster's botch is void and flimsy, the better to show that the Musician is the jack in office and can go to any length he pleases, even to making something out of nothing—the same as the good God! O how doubly dear and above all honor is Mozart to me, that it was not possible to him to invent music for *Tito* like that of *Don Giovanni*, for *Cosi fan Tutte* like that of *Figaro*! How shamefully would it have desecrated Music!

Soren Kierkegaard

(1813–1855) was born in Copenhagen, Denmark, spent all his life there, wrote extensively on ethical and moral themes and was much concerned about man's relations with God. His *Edifying Discourses* contain the many essays in which he attempts to come to grips with an overriding sense of guilt believed by commentators to have arisen from strained relations with his father.

From "Either/Or" in A Kierkegaard Anthology, ed. by Robert Bretall:

These two familiar strains of the violin! These two familiar strains here at this moment, in the middle of the street. Have I lost my senses? Does my ear, which from love of Mozart's music has ceased to hear, create these sounds; have the gods given me, unhappy beggar at the door of the temple—have they given me an ear that makes the sounds it hears? Only two strains, now I hear nothing more. Just as they burst forth from the deep choral tones of the immortal overture (to *Don Giovanni*), so here they extricate themselves from the noise and confusion of the street, with all the surprise of a revelation.

From "Stages on Life's Way" same anthology:

So long as one is a child one has sufficient imagination, though it were for an hour in a dark room, to keep one's soul on tiptoe, on the tiptoe of expectation; but when one is older, imagination easily has the effect of making one tired of the Christmas tree before one has a chance to see it.

The folding doors are thrown open; the effect of the radiant illumination, of the coolness which encountered them, of the infatuating fragrance of perfume, of the elegance of the table arrangement, overwhelmed for an instant the guests who were on the point of entering the room, and when at the same moment strains from the ballet of *Don Giovanni* reached them from the orchestra, they were transfixed and for an instant stood still as if in reverence

VIVA MOZART

before an invisible spirit which encompassed them, like a man whom admiration has awakened and who has risen to his feet to admire.

Only Victor stood somewhat apart, absorbed in his own thoughts; a shudder passed through him, he almost trembled; then, collecting himself, he saluted the prognostication (of a granted wish) in these words: "Ye secret, festive, seductive strains which tore me from the cloistered seclustion of my tranquil youth and beguiled me by a sense of loss, like a recollection, most terrible, as if Elvira had not been seduced at all but only desired to be! Immortal Mozart, to whom I owe all! But no, not yet do I owe thee all; but when I have become an old man, if ever I do, or when I am ten years older than now, if ever I come to that, or when I shall die, for of this at least I am certain, then I will say, Immortal Mozart, to whom I owe all! Then the admiration which is the first and only one I have known will suffer to break out with all its might, suffer it to slay me, as it often has threatened to do. Then I have set my house in order, then I have remembered my beloved, then I have confessed my love, then I have completely verified the fact that I owe thee all, then I belong to thee no more, no more belong to this world, but only to the solemn thought of death!"

GIUSEPPE VERDI

(1813–1901), acknowledged the greatest of Italian operatic composers, in 1832 failed examinations at the Milan Conservatory, but nevertheless became conductor of the Busseto Philharmonic and director of the Busseto school. After producing his first two operas, one of which failed, his *Nabucco* at La Scala (1842) made him an instant success and was followed by such masterpieces as *Ernani* (1844), *Rigoletto* (1851), *Il Trovatore* and *La Traviata* (both 1853) and *Aida* (1871). Toward the end of his life, in a remarkable burst of creative energy, he produced two more masterworks, *Otello* (1887) and *Falstaff* (1893).

From a letter to Giulio Ricordi, April 20, 1878:

> We cannot compose like the Germans, or at least we ought not to; nor they like us. Let the Germans assimilate our artistic substance, as Haydn and Mozart did in their time; yet they remained predominantly symphonic musicians. And it is perfectly proper for Rossini to have taken over certain formal elements from Mozart; he is still a melodist for all that.

CHARLES FRANCOIS GOUNOD

(1818–1893), one of France's greatest composers, was born in Paris and studied in the Paris Conservatory, winning the Prix de Rome in 1839. Back in Paris, he became organist at the Mission Etrangeres, lost interest in a church career and began the writing of opera, culminating in the production of *Faust* (1859) which confirmed his claim to greatness.

VIVA MOZART

From "Le Don Juan de Mozart" October 25, 1882:

Oh, divine Mozart! Hast thou reposed on the bosom of infinite beauty, as the beloved disciple reposed on the breast of Christ and drank in the incomparable grace which marks the great and privileged few? Did even your cradle hear those words which descended from on high, upon the Man of God transfigured: "This is my Beloved Son, in whom I am well pleased: Listen to him." Oh, yes, entirely pleased. For prodigal heaven gave thee everything, grace and strength, abundance and moderation, luminous spontaneity and ardent tenderness in the perfect equilibrium which constitutes the irresistible power to charm, and has made thee the unexcelled musician—more than the first—the only—Mozart! Who has run through the great gamut of human passions as he has done? Who has reached the extreme limits of the scale with the same infallible precision, equally guarded against the false refinement of artificial elegance and the roughness of spurious force? Who has better known how to breathe anguish and dread into the purest and most exquisite forms?

From "Composers on Music" regarding Don Giovanni:

Before describing the emotions that this incomparable masterpiece stirred in me, I ask myself if my pen can ever translate them—I do not say faithfully, since that seems to me impossible—but at least in such a way as to give some idea of what went on in me during those unparalleled hours, the charm of which has dominated my life like a luminous apparition, a kind of revelatory vision.

From the start of the overture I felt myself transported into an absolutely new world by the solemn and majestic chords of the Commandant's final scene. I was seized by a terror which froze me, and as the menacing progression began, with those descending and ascending scales unrolling above it, merciless and implacable as a death sentence, I was overcome by such dread that I buried my face in my mother's shoulder, and enveloped in the twofold embrace of the beautiful and the terrible, I whispered:

"Oh, mama, what music! this is truly music!"

Hearing Rossini's *Otello* had stirred the fibers of my musical instinct, but the impression which I got from *Don Giovanni* was of an altogether different significance and of quite another dimension. It seems to me that both impressions might be compared to those experienced by a painter who turns suddenly from the Venetian masters to Raphael, Leonardo da Vinci and Michelangelo. Rossini introduced me to purely musical delight; he charmed and fascinated my ear. Mozart did more; to the gratification deriving from the exclusively musical and sensuous, he added the profound and penetrating influence of truth of expression combined with perfect beauty. From beginning to end, the score was a long and inexpressible rapture—the pathetic tones of the trio at the Commandant's death, Donna Anna's lament over the body of her father, the grace of Zerlina and the consummate, masterful elegance of the trio of

Maskers, the trio which starts the second act under Elvira's balcony; in a word, everything (for this deathless work everything may be quoted) put me into that blessed state which one feels only before beautiful things to which the centuries must pay homage, things which are the yardstick of the aesthetic level of the arts. This performance counts as the loveliest experience of my childhood, and when, in 1839, I was awarded the *prix de Rome* my poor dear mother gave me the full score of *Don Giovanni* as a reward.

Ivan Turgenev

(1818–1883) was born in Orel, Russia of the gentry and studied liberal arts in Moscow and St. Petersburg before setting out for Berlin in 1834 where he lived and worked until 1841, greatly influenced by 'western' thought. His first writings won immediate success but later his liberal leanings earned him exile at his home estate, Spasskoye, where he wrote his most famous novels, *Rudin* (1856), *A Nest of Gentle Folk* (1859) and *Fathers and Sons* (1862). He spent the rest of his life in Baden-Baden and Paris where his last two novels were written, *Smoke* (1867) and *Virgin Soil* (1877).

From "Fathers and Sons":

"Kayta raised the top of the piano, and not looking at Arkady, she said in a low voice:

"What am I to play for you?"

"What you like," answered Arkady indifferently.

"What sort of music do you like best?" repeated Katya, without changing her attitude.

"Classical," Arkady answered in the same tone of voice.

"Do you like Mozart?"

"Yes, I like Mozart."

Katya pulled out Mozart's Sonata-Fantasia in C minor. She played very well, though rather over correctly and precisely. She sat upright and immovable, her eyes fixed on the notes, and her lips tightly compressed, only at the end of the sonata her face glowed, her hair came loose, and a little lock fell on to her dark brow

Arkady was particularly struck by the last part of the sonata, the part in which, in the midst of the bewitching gaiety of the careless melody, the pangs of such mournful, almost tragic suffering, suddenly break in. . . . But the ideas stirred in him by Mozart's music had no reference to Katya. Looking at her, he simply thought, "Well, that young lady doesn't play badly, and she's not bad-looking either."

When she had finished the sonata, Katya, without taking her hands from the keys, asked, "Is that enough?" Arkady declared that he could not venture to trouble her again, and began talking to her about Mozart; he asked her whether she had chosen that sonata herself, or some one had recommended it to her. But Katya answered him in monosyllables; she withdrew into herself, went back into her shell."

From "Smoke":

. . . the humblest German flute-player, modestly blowing his part in the humblest German orchestra, has twenty times as many ideas as all our untaught geniuses; only the flute-player keeps his ideas to himself, and doesn't trot them out with a flourish in the land of Mozarts and Haydns.

Henri Frederic Amiel

(1821–1881), born in Geneva, Switzerland, was a teacher and diarist of whom great literary achievement was expected. Professor of Philosophy at the University of Geneva from 1854 until his death, he never married and wrote little. The year after he died, friends published selections from his voluminous diaries, *Fragments d'un Journal Intime*, that has become his masterwork, regarded in the Nineteenth Century as almost equal to Rousseau's *Confessions*.

From "Amiel's Journal" translated by Mrs. Humphrey Ward, London, 1899, an entry of May 14, 1853:

The quartets were perfectly clear and easy to understand. One was by Mozart and the other by Beethoven, so that I could compare the two masters. Their individuality seemed to become plain to me: Mozart—grace, certainty, freedom, and precision of style,—the health and talent of master, both on a level with his genius: Beethoven—more pathetic, more passionate, more torn with feeling, more intricate, more profound, less perfect, more the slave of his genius, more carried away by his fancy or his passion, more moving and more sublime than Mozart. Mozart refreshes you like the Dialogues of Plato: he respects you, reveals to you your strength, gives you freedom and balance. Beethoven seizes upon you: he is more tragic and oratorical, while Mozart is more disinterested and poetical. Mozart is more Greek, and Beethoven more Christian. One is serene, the other serious. The first is stronger than destiny, because he takes life less profoundly: the second is less strong, because he has dared to measure himself against deeper sorrows. His talent is not always equal to his genius, and pathos is his dominant feature, as perfection is that of Mozart. In Mozart the balance of the whole is perfect, and art triumphs: in Beethoven feeling governs everything, and emotion troubles his art in proportion as it deepens it.

BEDRICH SMETANA

(1824–1884), born in Leitomischl, Bohemia, is best known for his opera, *The Bartered Bride* (1866) but is also regarded as the founder of his country's serious music, exemplified by the tone poem *Ma Vlast* (1874–1879). Like Beethoven, he became deaf in the last years of his life and near the end went insane.

From "Bedrich Smetana—Letters and Reminiscences" by Frantisek Bartos, Artia, Prague 1953:

(Smetana's diary entry of January 23, 1843) . . . By the grace of God and with His help I shall one day be a Liszt in technique, in composition a Mozart.

(recollection of Ferdinand Heller): To the question what he considered to be the height of original expression he (Smetana) answered: "When it is possible to say after a few bars: that is Mozart—that is Chopin. Of other composers, less original, it is impossible to say as much often even after a hundred bars, indeed sometimes after the entire work . . ."

(Letter from Goteborg to Franz Liszt, April 10, 1857): Economically I am in a much better position than in Prague, as I am literally inundated with lessons; but musically I am completely isolated, not only because of a dearth of musical communication, but also because of a lack of direction. The people here are still solidly fixed in an antediluvian artistic point of view. Mozart is their idol, though he is not really understood, Beethoven feared, Mendelssohn declared unplayable, and the moderns unknown.

LEO N. TOLSTOY

(1828–1910) was born on his parents' estate, Yasnaya Polyana, south of Moscow, grew up at his aunt's home (both parents having died while he was still a child) and was educated at home by tutors. He enrolled at Kazan University in Oriental languages, expelled in a year for lack of interest, then began studying law at the same school. After a few years of dissolute life here, he entered the Imperial Army and while there wrote his *Childhood* (1852) and *Sevastopol Sketches* (1856). Back at Yasnaya Polyana in 1862 he married an 18 year old girl of noble birth; she bore him 18 children. Now followed the production of his two great masterpeices, *War and Peace* (1869) and *Anna Karenina* (1876), perhaps the greatest narrative fictions ever written. In later years, obsessed with the problem of existence and seeking its meaning, he produced essays and tracts that made of him a worldwide cult figure.

From "The Kreutzer Sonata":

"They (Kreutzer's wife and her love) played a few things, some songs without words, and a little sonata by Mozart. They played splendidly, and he had an exceptionally fine tone. Besides that, he had a refined and elevated taste not at all in correspondence with his character."

Anton Rubinstein

(1829–1894), born in Vykhvatinets, Russia, early displayed great pianistic talent and was taken to Paris at age 10 where he played for Liszt and Chopin, and soon launched a successful touring career. He composed extensively but perhaps his most lasting contribution to music was the founding of the St. Petersburg Conservatory in 1862.

From "A Conversation on Music" published by Chas. F. Tretbar, New York, 1892:

Madame von———honors me with a visit at my villa in Peterhof; after the usual salutations she expresses a wish to inspect my home surroundings; in the music-room she notices the busts of J.S. Bach, Beethoven, Schubert, Chopin and Glinka on the walls, and, greatly surprised, asks:
"Why only these and not also Handel, Haydn, Mozart and others?"

"These are the ones whom I most revere in my art."

"Then you do not revere Mozart?"

"Himalaya and Chimborazo are the highest peaks of the earth; that does not imply, however, that Mt. Blanc is a little mountain."

"But Mozart is generally considered this highest point of which you speak! He has indeed given us in his Operas the highest of which music is capable."

"To me the Opera is altogether a subordinate branch of our art."

"Just as Haydn, as the *old Haydn*, becomes a type, so Mozart, as the *young Mozart*, may be called a type. Although as to his age and surroundings, standing on the same level of culture with Haydn, he is young, sincere, tender in everything; the journeys of his childhood also had an influence on his musical thoughts and feeling. In consequence the Opera became his chief work, but his entire *Ego* gives us in his instrumental works, and there I hear him too, like Haydn, speak the Vienna dialect. Helios of music I would call him! He has illuminated all forms of music with his splendor, on one and all impressed this stamp of the god-like. We are at a loss which to admire most in him, his melody or his technic, his crystal clearness or the richness of his invention. The symphony in G minor (this *unicum* of symphonic lyric), the last movement of the "Jupiter" Symphony (this *unicum* in symphonic technic), the overtures to the "Zauberflote," or to "Figaro" (these *unicum* of the merry, the fresh, the god-like), the Requiem (this *unicum* of sweet tone-in-sorrow), the Pianoforte Fantasias, the String Quintette in G minor; in the latter it is not uninteresting to see verified how greatly wealth of melody outweighs everything else in music. We demand generally in quartette style a polyphonic treatment of the voices; here however homeophony reigns, the very simplest accompaniment to every theme that enters—and we revel in the enjoyment of this divine melodiad, and at last, besides all these, the wonderful instrumental works, the wonderful operas! Gluck, it is true, had achieved great things in the opera before him; yea, opened new paths—but in comparison with Mozart he is, so to say, of stone. Besides, Mozart has the merit of having removed the opera from the icy pathos of mythology into real life, into the purely human, and from the Italian to the German language, and thereby to a national path. The most remarkable feature of his operas is the musical characteristic he has given to every figure so that each acting personage has become an immortal type. It is true that the happy choice of material and its excellent scenic treatment was of great assistance in this."

"The text to the *Magic Flute* is generally considered childish and ludicrous?"

"I hold a contrary opinion—even if it were only on account of the variety it offers to the musician. Pathetic, fantastic, lyric, comic, naive, romantic, dramatic, tragic, yes, it would be hard to find an expression that is wanting in it. The case is the same in *Don Juan*. It is evident the genius of Mozart was required to reproduce all musically as he has done;

VIVA MOZART

but such Opera texts might incite less genial composers to interesting work."

"But that which *he* has made, he alone could make!"

"Yes, a god-like creation—all flooded with light. In hearing Mozart I always wish to exclaim: 'Eternal sunshine in music, thy name is Mozart!'"

"It is incomprehensible to me how you, while giving him such exalted admiration, still do not give him the highest recognition."

"Mankind thirsts for a storm—it feels it may become dry and parched in the Eternal Haydn-Mozart sunshine; it wishes to express itself earnestly, it longs for action, it becomes dramatic, the French revolution breaks forth—Beethoven appears!"

". . . I do not believe, as is generally said today, that Mozart wrote for the Spinet—the orchestration of his Pianoforte Concertos makes that improbable, also the five octave compass of his Pianoforte compositions. It is possible that he had a Spinet in his work room, but publicly he must have played upon a beautiful toned Grand Piano. The pinched, short, small tone of the Spinet known to us would not allow the brilliancy of the *passage* or the wonderful charm of his melody in his compositions, it must be, then, that the instrument a hundred years ago had an entirely different tone from the one we hear from it today."

"In your opinion then, the Pianoforte of our day is no advance?"

"No advance in the sense of works *before* the time of Beethoven. I would like to recommend a different use (touch and pedal) of the Pianoforte of our day, in playing the compositions of different epochs. So for example I would play a piece of Haydn or Mozart on the instrument of our day, especially in '*forte*' with the left pedal, because their '*forte*' has not the character of the Beethoven '*forte*,' especially not of the latest composers. Playing Handel and especially Bach, I would try by means of variety of touch and change of pedal to register, that is, give them throughout an organ-like character . . ."

EMILY DICKINSON

(1830–1886), of Amherst, Massachusetts, early learned to play the piano, and spent much of her life reclusively, writing her cryptic poetry which deals with the great themes of nature, love and death. Her poems, not widely known until after her death, are among the most original and seminal written in America, rivaling Whitman's in originality and considered by many the greatest yet produced.

circa 1862

> Better—than Music! For I—who heard it—
> I was used—to the Birds—before—
> This was different—'Twas Translation—
> Of all tunes I knew—and more—
>
> 'Twasn't contained—like other stanza—
> No one could play it—the second time—
> But the Composer—perfect Mozart—
> Perish with him—that Keyless Rhyme!

So—Children—told how Brooks in Eden—
Bubbled a better—Melody—
Quaintly infer—Eve's great surrender—
Urging the feet—that would—not—fly—

Children—matured—are wiser—mostly—
Eden—a legend—dimly told—
Eve—and the Anguish—Grandma's story—
But—I was telling a tune—I heard—

Not such a strain—the Church—baptizes—
When the last Saint—goes up the Aisles—
Not such a stanza splits the silence—
When the Redemption strikes her Bells—

Let me not spill—its smallest cadence—
Humming—for promise—when alone—
Humming—until my faint Rehearsal—
Drop into tune—around the Throne—

Joseph Joachim

(1831–1907) born in Kittsee, Hungary, took to the violin as a child of 5 and throughout his life made that instrument his trademark. After Paganini he was probably the world's most celebrated violinist though he has several songs, orchestral and solo works to his credit.

From "Letters to and from Joseph Joachim" selected and translated by Nora Bickley. Macmillan & Co. London, 1914:

To Bernhard Cossmann, dated September 16, 1853.

The Opera (Cherubini's *Wassertrager*) left me cold in spite of many musical and even dramatic beauties; it even bored me at times. I was amazed to find how much I must have altered since a few years ago when so many things in it delighted me. Now I seem to miss more especially the natural, joyous something which, in Mozart's most antiquated forms, charms us with its eternal youth. Doubtless Cherubini also experienced emotions and he has expressed them in his music, but like one who has been incommoded rather than inspired by them.

To Gisela von Arnim, dated May 19, 1856.

In the evening I heard the most beautiful and charming Italian voice I have ever come across, as Zerlina in *Don Juan*. The singer was called Borghi Mamo; if Mozart had ever been able to spirit his music into a throat instead of writing it on music paper, it would have sounded like that. Delightful; not a breath too many, and yet so full and soft. Indeed, the whole opera made a greater impression on me than ever, in spite of the mediocre orchestra, because the characters were alive, and particularly because the freedom of movement was expressed by the *rhythm* of the singing; Germans often neglect this point. In this case you readily forgot that much in it was not ideal enough, just because there was a natural element in it all, which gave Mozart's indestructible grace free play. I never understood Mozart's genius for opera writing so well before and kept thinking affectionately of him whilst I was in Vienna.

JOHANNES BRAHMS'

(1833–1897) father played double bass in the Hamburg Opera orchestra and taught his son, who at age 14 gave his first piano concert. Born in Hamburg, Brahms entered into the stream of German romanticism, proud of his German heritage and very mindful of the great masters of the symphonic form who preceded him. He did not produce work in that form until 1868 with *Variations on a Theme by Haydn* and his *First Symphony* in 1876, after which he was generally regarded as the musical successor of Beethoven.

From a letter by Brahms to Heinrich Herzogenberg in which Brahms refers first to Schumann's D Minor Symphony (October 1886):

The original scoring has always delighted me. It is a real pleasure to see anything so bright and spontaneous expressed with corresponding ease and grace. It reminds me (without comparing it in other respects) of Mozart's G Minor, the score of which I also possess. Everything is so absolutely natural that you cannot imagine it different; there are no harsh colors, no forced effects, and so on.

From a conversation the conductor Joseph Joachim had with Brahms, reported by ——— Abell:

"Measure by measure, the finished product is revealed to me when I am in those rare, inspired moods, as they were to Tartini when he composed his greatest work—the Devil's Trill Sonata. I have to be in a semi-trance condition to get such results—a condition when the conscious mind is in temporary abeyance and the subconscious is in control, for it is through the subconscious mind, which is a part of Omnipotence, that the inspiration comes. I have to be careful, however, not to lose consciousness, otherwise the ideas fade away.   That is the way Mozart composed. He was once asked what the process was with him while composing and he replied:

'Es geht bei mir zu wie in einem schonen, starken Traume.' (The process with me is like a vivid dream).

He then went on and described how ideas, clothed in the proper musical setting, streamed down upon him, just as they do with me. Of course, a composer must have mastered the technic of composition, form, theory, harmony, counterpoint, instrumentation—but any musical person can do that if he has the proper application. Although I must say, that to acquire a mastery of the orchestra such as my young friend Richard Strauss has, requires exceptional ability. Mark my word, Joseph, he will go far."

From Mozart in Retrospect *by A. Hyatt King in a letter to Anton Dvorak:*

If we cannot write with the beauty of Mozart, let us at least try to write with his purity.

Quoted by Guido Adler in his biography of Mahler:

No one does *Don Giovanni* the way I like it. If I wish to enjoy it, I lie down on the sofa and read the score, but after hearing Mahler's conducting of the opera in Budapest, Brahms said, "Excellent! Splendid! Magnificent! Yes, that's it, finally. What a devil of a fellow!"

CHARLES-CAMILLE SAINT-SAENS

(1835–1921), born in Paris, concertized at the piano at age 4 and wrote music at age 6. At 18 he began a long career as organist and piano virtuoso, wrote concertos for the latter that are often performed today, while his great contribution to opera was *Samson and Delilah* (1877). France honored him throughout his long life and awarded him the Grand Croix in the Legion of Honor.

From "Composers on Music" by Sam Morganstern:

Give Mozart a fairy tale, and he creates without effort an immortal masterpiece.

If it were not for Mozart's music, the puppets of the *Magic Flute* would amount to nothing.

What gives Sebastian Bach and Mozart a place apart is that these two great expressive composers never sacrificed form to expression. As high as their expression may soar, their musical form remains supreme and all-sufficient.

Georges Bizet

(1838–1875) was born in Paris of a musical father (vocal teacher) and mother (pianist) who began his musical instruction at age 4. At 10 he entered the Conservatory and won the Prix de Rome at 19. Today his *Carmen* (1875) is probably one of the best known operas in the world though not in Bizet's lifetime. His *Pearl Fishers* (1863), *L'Arlesienne Suite* (1872) and other works put him firmly in the Pantheon of French composers.

From "Bizet and His World" by Mina Curtiss:

"Mozart's *Requiem* fills me with admiration."

"Comparisons between painters and sculptors and musicians are useful. All the arts are related, or rather there is only one art. Whether one expresses one's thought on canvas, in marble, or on the stage matters little; the thinking is always the same. I am more than ever convinced that Mozart and Rossini are the two greatest musicians. While I admire Beethoven and Meyerbeer mightily, I feel that my nature tends to make me like pure and *spontaneous* art more than the passionately dramatic. So in painting Raphael is the same man as Mozart."

"Up to this moment I floated between Mozart and Beethoven, Rossini and Meyerbeer. Now I know what to adore. There are two kinds of genius: natural genius and rational genius. While I admire the second tremendously, I shall not disguise the fact that I am wholly drawn to the first. Yes, *mon cher*, I have the courage to prefer Raphael to Michelangelo, Mozart to Beethoven, and Rossini to Meyerbeer . . . It is a matter of taste; one order of ideas influences and attracts my nature more strongly than the other. When I look at *The Last Judgement*, when I hear the *Eroica* or the fourth act of *Les Huguenots*, I am moved, surprised, and haven't eyes, ears, brains enough to admire them. But when I look at *The School of Athens, The Dispute of the Holy Sacrament,* the *Virgin of Foligno,* when I hear *Le Nozze di Figaro* or the second act of *Guillaume Tell,* I am completely happy, I experience a well-being, a complete satisfaction that makes me forget everything else."

"A man can be a great artist without having the *motif,* then he must renounce money and popular success. But he can also be better than other men and possess this precious gift; witness Rossini. Rossini is the greatest of all because, like Mozart, he has all the virtues—elevation, style, and finally . . . the *motif.*"

"It takes a lot of strength to be an artist. It is hard, very hard indeed, particularly in Rome. The wind of the sirocco has an unheard-of effect on the nerves. You know me, and you know that I haven't at all a nervous temperament. Well, on the days when the sirocco blows, I can't touch *Don Giovanni* or *Le Nozze* or *Cosi fan tutte*. Mozart's music affects me so directly that it actually makes me very sick. Certain of Rossini's works produce the same effect."

"Don't talk about method to a musician; what you call 'scholarly music' is merely awkwardly put together. (I am speaking generally.) Mozart and Rossini both had the most prodigious talent imaginable. When they were inspired they created *Don Giovanni, The Magic Flute, The Barber of Seville* (a little dated), *Guillaume Tell.* With talent alone they created all those boring symphonies, *Semiramide,* almost all of *Otello,* etc., etc., etc."

Thomas Hardy

(1840–1928) author of *The Return of the Native, Tess of the D'Urbervilles,* and other novels, set in his mythical Wessex, was also a poet influential in modern English poetry, early played the violin, mostly in country musicals, and was a keen concert goer in Victorian London. His poetry is characterized by idiosyncratic word usage and a dark view of man's fate but suffused by pity and compassion.

Poem in "Moments of Vision" (1917):

LINES

To a Movement in Mozart's E-Flat Symphony

>Show me again the time
>When in the Junetide's prime
>We flew by meads and mountains northerly!—
>Yea, to such freshness, fairness, fulness, fineness, freeness,
>Love lures life on.

>   Show me again the day
>   When from the sandy bay
>   We looked together upon the pestered sea!—
> Yea, to such surging, swaying, sighing, swelling,
>   shrinking,
>   Love lures life on.
>
>   Show me again the hour
>   When by the pinnacled tower
>   We eyed each other and feared futurity!—
> Yea, to such bodings, broodings, beatings,
>   blanchings, blessings,
>   Love lures life on.
>
>   Show me again just this:
>   The moment of that kiss
>   Away from the prancing folk, by the strawberry
>   tree!—
> Yea, to such rashness, ratheness, rareness, ripeness,
>   richness,
>   Love lures life on.

PETER ILYTCH TCHAIKOVSKY

(1840–1893), born in Votkinsk, Russia, began a career in the Ministry of Justice, but his innate musical talent soon led to study at the St. Petersburg Conservatory where he immediately showed his musical genius and composed his *First Symphony* (1866) and the *Romeo and Juliet* fantasy (1869). After a brief disastrous marriage he settled down to composition and a 13-year epistolary association with a patroness, Nadezhda von Meck (whom he never saw) and became one of the recognized leading composers of his country. He was of morbid temperament which is reflected in most of his music, especially in his last great symphony, the *Pathetique* (1893).

From a letter to Nadezhda Filaretovna von Meck, from Clarens, March 28, 1878:

Why don't you like Mozart? In this our opinions differ, dear friend. I not only like Mozart, I worship him. To me the most beautiful opera ever written is *Don Giovanni*. You, who have such fine taste in music, must surely love this pure and ideal artist.

It is true that Mozart used his gift too generously and often wrote without inspiration because he was compelled to do so by poverty. But read his biography by Otto Jahn and you will see he could not help it. Even Bach and Beethoven have left a considerable number of inferior works, not worthy of being mentioned in the same breath as their masterpieces. Occasionally Fate compelled them to lower their art to the level of a handicraft. But think of Mozart's operas, of two or three of his symphonies, his Requiem, the six quartets dedicated to Haydn, and the G-minor String Quintet. Do you feel no charm in these works?

True, Mozart reaches neither the depths nor the heights of Beethoven; his range is not so wide. And since in life, too, he remained a careless child to the end of his days, his music does not have that subjectively tragic quality which is expressed so powerfully in Beethoven. But this did not prevent him from creating an objectively tragic type, the most superb and wonderful human presentation ever depicted in music. I mean Donna Anna in *Don Giovanni.* Oh, how difficult it is to make anyone see and feel in music what we see and feel ourselves! I am quite incapable of describing to you what I felt on hearing *Don Giovanni,* especially the scene where the noble figure of the beautiful, proud, revengeful woman appears on the stage. Nothing in any opera has ever impressed me so deeply. Afterwards when Donna Anna recognizes in Don Giovanni the man who has wounded her pride and killed her father, and her anger bursts out like a rushing torrent in that magnificent recitative, and that aria later on, when every note of the orchestra seems to speak of her wrath and pride and actually quiver with horror—I could cry out and weep from the overpowering strain on the emotions. And her lament over her father's body, the duet with Don Ottavio where she swears vengeance, her arioso in the great sextet in the churchyard—these are incomparable, superb operatic scenes!

I love the music of *Don Giovanni* so much that even as I write you I could shed tears of agitation and emotion. In his chamber music Mozart fascinates me by his purity and distinction of style and his exquisite handling of the parts. Here, too, there are things that bring tears to our eyes. I shall mention only the adagio of the G-minor String Quintet. No one else has ever known how to interpret so beautifully and exquisitely in music the feeling of resignation and inconsolable sorrow. Every time Laub (a violinist) played the adagio I had to hide in the farthest corner of the concert room so that others would not see how much this music affected me.

I could go on speaking interminably about that radiant genius whom I worship. Though I am used to considerable variety of taste in music, and though I certainly appreciate freedom from authority, I must confess, my dear, that I should like very much to convert you to Mozart. I know that would be difficult. I have known some other people who also understood and loved music very much but did not recognize Mozart. I have tried in vain to open up to them the beauty in his music, but never have I wished to convert anyone into a Mozart-admirer so much as I now want to convert you.

Frequently chance circumstances influence our musical preferences. The music of *Don Giovanni* was the first music to produce an overwhelming effect on me and it aroused in me a holy ecstasy that bore fruit later on. Through it I entered the realm of artistic beauty where only the greatest geniuses dwell. Until that time I had known only Italian opera. Mozart is responsible for my having dedicated my life to music. He gave the first impetus to my musical strength; he made me love music more than anything else in the world. That may have great significance in my exclusive love of Mozart, and I cannot require everyone I love to feel the same way toward him. But if I can somehow help change your opinion of him, I shall be very happy. I should be delighted if some day, for example, after listening to the Adagio in the G-minor, you would write me that you were moved.

Now I must ask your forgiveness for speaking at such length about Mozart. But how could I not want my dear, best, incomparable friend to worship the one I worship over all musicians? How could I not try to make you feel moved and carried away by that music which makes me tremble with indescribable bliss?

From Tchaikovsky's "Diaries" (1886):

Probably after my death it will not be uninteresting to know what were my musical predilections and prejudices, especially since I seldom gave opinions in verbal conversation . . . Shall start with Beethoven. . . . I bow before the greatness of some of his works—but I do not *love* Beethoven. My attitude toward him reminds me of what I experienced in childhood toward the God Jehovah. I had toward Him (and even now my feelings have not changed) a feeling of wonder, but at the same time also of fear. He created Heaven and earth, He too created me—and still even though I bow before Him, there is no *love*. Christ, on the contrary, inspires truly and exclusively the feeling of *love*. Though He was *God,* He was at the same time man. He suffered like us. We *pity* Him, we love Him His ideal *human* side, and if Beethoven occupies a place in my heart analogous to the God Jehovah, then Mozart I love as the musical Christ. Incidentally, he lived almost as long as Christ. I think that there is nothing sacrilegious in this comparison. Mozart was a being so angelic, so childlike, so pure; his music is so full of unapproachable, divine beauty, that if anyone could be named with Christ, then it is he.

Speaking of Beethoven, I come to Mozart. According to my deep conviction, Mozart is the highest, the culminating point that *beauty* has attained in the sphere of music. No one has made me weep, has made me tremble with rapture, from the consciousness of my nearness to *that something* which we call the *ideal,* as he has done.

Beethoven also made me tremble. But rather from something like fear and the pangs of suffering.

I cannot *discourse* on music and shall not go into details. However, I shall mention two details: (1) In Beethoven I love the middle period, at times the first, but I fundamentally *detest* the last, especially the last quartets. Here there are *glimmers*—and nothing more. The rest is *chaos,* over which, surrounded by an impenetrable fog, hovers the spirit of this musical Jehovan. (2) In Mozart I love *everything,* for we love *everything* in a person whom we love truly. Above all *Don Juan,* for thanks to it I learned what *music* is. Until that time (until my seventeenth year) I did not know any music except Italian, semi-music, however charming. Of course, loving everything in Mozart, I shall not start asserting that every insignificant work of his is a *chef-d'oeuvre*. Yes! I know that none of his sonatas, for example, is a great work, and *still* I love every one of his sonatas because it is *his,* because this musical Christ imprinted it with his serene touch.

Concerning the forerunners of both, can say that I play Bach gladly, for to play a good fugue is entertaining, but I do not recognize in him (as some do) a great genius. Handel has for me an entirely fourth-rate significance and he is not even entertaining. Gluck, despite the relative poverty of his creation, is attractive to me. I *like* certain things of Haydn. But all these four Muses are amalgamated in Mozart. He who knows Mozart also knows what is good in these four, because being the greatest and most potent of all musical creators, he was not averse, even, to taking them under his wings and saving them from oblivion. They are rays lost in the sun of Mozart.

ANTONIN DVORAK

(1841–1904) born in Prague, was a musically talented boy who studied at the Prague Organ School and became an accomplished violinist in the National Theatre Orchestra while composing steadily. His symphonies and concertos for piano, violin and cello are staples of today's repertories. His *Symphony No. 9* "From the New World" (1893) exploits American Negro melodies Dvorak heard during his tenure as director of the National Conservatory of Music in New York. He returned to Prague in 1895 as Director of the Prague Conservatory a post he held until his death.

From "Dvorak" by John Clapham:

Dvorak quoted in the *New York Herald,* January 14, 1884:

Mozart! Ah, Mozart is the greatest of them all. Beethoven is grand. His works are always sublime in conception and sublime in working out. But it is awe that he inspires, while Mozart touches my heart. His melodies are so lovable, are so inspired and so inspiring, that only to hear them is the greatest enjoyment that exists in the world for me. Schubert also has somewhat of Mozart's qualities so far as impressing me is concerned.

(Dvorak's) memorial service (May 7, 1904) took place at the Tyn church (Prague) where they sang the Requiem Mass of Mozart, the composer who reminded Dvorak of sunshine, and whom he thought of when he saw a Raphael madonna in London.

SIDNEY LANIER

(1842–1881) grew up in the state of Georgia and from age 7 played musical instruments, but after graduating from Oglethorpe University, enrolled in the Confederate Army and from experiences there wrote a novel *Tiger-Lilies,* and thereafter dedicated his life to writing poetry.

From a manuscript fragment in his Collected Works (quoted in "Pleasures of Music" ed. by Jacques Barzun:

All shades in an American audience; from those who cry give us a tune, something quick and devilish, to those who find in music a religion of emotions and a comfort and triumph in the darkest hour of the soul. Composers must not be characterized. We must not take Beethoven and Mozart and stick a pin through each one like so many bugs and butterflies in a glass case, and say this one Beethoven belongs to the class of big beetles (Coleoptera gigans) and Mozart to the class of butterflies (———!). If we do, the composers will become as dry and dusty as an entomologist's collections.

SIR ARTHUR SULLIVAN

(1842–1900), born in London, his fame is associated with the name of W.S. Gilbert who wrote the lyrics for the most popular operettas ever written and that are still constantly produced, including *H. M. S. Pinafore* (1878), *The Mikado* (1885), *The Pirates of Penzance* (1879) and many others. Sullivan's other well-known works include the hymns, *Nearer My God to Thee* (1872) and *Rock of Ages* (1867).

From "Sir Arthur Sullivan" by Herbert Sullivan and Newman Flower:

(Travelling with George Grove) to Munich, Salzburg and the memories of Mozart. Sullivan and Grove followed Mozart's footsteps through the city, ardent with reverence.

"We went and saw the house Mozart was born and lived in," Sullivan wrote to his mother, "and the Mozartium where all relics of him are preserved. Both his harpsichords, various portraits and many letters and manuscripts are here. When we wrote our names in the Visitors' Book the librarian asked me if I was the composer of whom he had often read in the 'Signale' and other musical papers. I modestly owned that I did occasionally write a little music, and we bowed and complimented each other.

Edvard Hagerup Grieg

(1843–1907) was born in Bergen, Norway and received a thorough musical education in Leipzig and Copenhagen. He was a founder of the Norwegian Academy of Music and championed the cause of generic Norwegian music. His *Peer Gynt* (1876), *Norwegian Dances* (1881) and *Holberg Suite* (1844) plus the *A Minor Piano Concerto* (1869) brought him international fame and fortune.

From an article by Grieg in "The Century Magazine," November, 1897:

"What kind of face would Bach, Handel, Haydn and Mozart make after hearing an opera by Wagner?" asks an English writer. I shall not attempt to answer for the first three, but it is safe to say that Mozart, the universal genius whose mind was free from Philistinism and one-sidedness, would not only open his eyes wide, but would be as delighted as a child with all the new acquisitions in the departments of drama and orchestra. In this light must Mozart be viewed . . . Where he is greatest, he embraces all times.

In Bach, Beethoven and Wagner we admire principally the depth and energy of the human mind; in Mozart, the divine instinct. His highest inspirations seem untouched by human labor. Unlike the masters cited, no trace of struggle remains in the forms in which he molded his material. Mozart has the childish, happy, Aladdin nature which overcomes all difficulties as in play. He creates like a god, without pain . . .

His early and perfect mastery of the technic of composition suggests an interesting comparison with Wagner. Both of these masters won immortality with their operas. Both threw themselves with all the enthusiasm of youth into this branch of art. Wagner's experience, acquired by early activity as a conductor, has its counterpart in the strict training Mozart received through his travels, begun in childhood as a musician. The result in each case is clearness. Both these musicians are from the outset complete masters of the complicated apparatus required for the writing of an opera—an apparatus most composers learn to control only by long and laborious effort, with hard struggles and disappointments. Let us place the two juvenile masterworks, *The Abduction from the Seraglio* and *Tannhauser* side by side. There is no wavering in either, but perfect certainty in aim and in choice of means. On the basis of this technical mastership, the individuality of each master develops with wonderful rapidity. The step from *Tannhauser* to *Lohengrin* is just as great as that from the *Abduction* to *Figaro*! The warm light of fully conscious personality is diffused from every bar of these two masterworks. If we review further the creative activity of their composers, what melancholy seizes us in contemplating Mozart's fate! All the principal works of Wagner were yet to be written; also it is true, the two greatest of Mozart's—*Don Giovanni* and *The Magic Flute*; but after these his life was cut short at the beginning of his manhood. The death of Mozart before he had passed his thirty-fifth year is perhaps the greatest loss the musical world has ever suffered . . . To his last hour his genius continued to develop. In *The Magic Flute* and the *Requiem* we have a presentiment that new hidden springs are on the point of bursting forth. That Mozart learned to know and love Bach so late in his life must be regarded as a leading circumstance in connection with this fact. With what deep fervor he allowed this man to strike root in his own personality, we see, among other things, in the delightful fugued choral in the last act of *The Magic Flute*. It was Wagner's polyphonic power that secured him his later triumphs; and this same power would have led Mozart to new victories if he could have been permitted to live longer. For it was this power which, notwithstanding the influence of the Italian school, lay in the depth of his German soul, and which Bach first helped him to find in the privacy of his own personality.

When we compare Mozart and Wagner, the truth of the proverb that 'extremes meet' forces itself upon us. That these two masters represented the 'extremes' is easily understood by any lover of music, but it may perhaps be necessary to indicate where they 'meet.' Truly Weber may be regarded as Wagner's predecessor; but if Gluck is named, and not improperly, as the man on whose shoulders Wagner stands, then we must not forget how much he owes to Mozart. For the greatness of Mozart lies in the fact that his influence in the dramatic part of music extends to our time. I have in mind, for example, the developed recitative where Mozart more and more trod paths which it remained for Wagner to develop in his dialogue still further for the modern music drama. Certain recitatives of Donna Anna and Elvira in *Don Giovanni* are the originals after which our whole conception of the recitative has been molded.

From "Edvard Grieg" by David Monrad-Johansen. Translated by Madge Robertson:

In a letter of April 23, 1877, he (Grieg) tells what exactly he has been doing in the way of composition: "In my free time lately I have been busy composing 'piano secundo' to the Mozart piano sonatas and have just tried it over with Fru Lie-Nissen. Much of it sounded very fine—so fine that I have grounds for hoping that Mozart will not 'turn in his grave.' "

And to his publisher Dr. Abraham he wrote on May 27: "Ich habe im Winter eine Arbeit vorgehabt, was mich interessierte; namlich ein freis, zweites Piano zu mehreren Sonaten von Mozart hinzu komponiert. Die Arbeit war zunachst fur den Unerricht bestimmt, kam aber zufalligerweise in den Konzertsaal und die Geschichte klang uberraschend gut."

Grieg has been criticized for his "manipulation" of Mozart, and, from a strictly artistic point of view, criticism is justified. The best one can say of manipulations of this sort is that they are unnecessary. And to provide work so sparklingly clear and so full of delicate feelings as Mozart's with needless duplications and paddings is a dangerous thing to do. But from his letter to Dr. Abraham, it would appear that it was with teaching in his mind that Grieg began the work. Nor would he ever have intended that this "opus" should come to be reckoned among his works, as has actually happened owing to the way in which it was sold and dealt with by the publishers. But there came a time when everything with Grieg's name on it had acquired an undreamt-of value.

From an essay on Mozart, quoted in "Composers of Yesterday" by David Ewen:

Edvard Grieg, the famous composer, has written an illuminating essay on Mozart which is not widely known. In it, he has discussed Mozart's greatest symphonies in the following manner: "We note at once the great step from Haydn's to Mozart's treatment of this highest of instrumental forms (the symphony), and our thoughts are involuntarily transferred to the young Beethoven who, without any specially noteworthy break, rises from where Mozart left off to those proud summits which none but he was destined to reach. In the introduction of the E-flat major Symphony, just before the first allegro, we come upon harmonic combinations of unprecedented boldness. They are introduced in so surprising a way that they will always preserve the impression of novelty ... In the G-minor Symphony, Mozart shows himself to us in all his grace and sincerity of feeling. It is worth noting what astonishing effects he gets here by the use of chromatic progressions. In the Jupiter Symphony we are astounded, above all, by the playful ease with which the greatest problems of art are treated. No one who is not initiated suspects in the finale, amid the humorous tone gambols, what an amazing contrapuntal knowledge and superiority Mozart manifests. And then this ocean of euphony! Mozart's sense of euphony was, indeed, so absolute that it is impossible, in all his works, to find a single bar wherein it is sacrificed to other considerations."

HENRY JAMES

(1843–1916) was born in Washington Place, New York, son of a noted theologian of the same name, into a wealthy family which included his famous philosopher brother William and a gifted sister Alice. He was educated at schools in London, Paris and Geneva, and in 1865 began writing short stories and reviews. Living alternately in Europe and America, his early fiction reflected his interest in the differences in these cultures, but he finally settled in England and before his death became a British citizen. Considered one of the great novelists writing in English, his masterpieces, many agree, are the carefully structured and painstakingly elaborate psychological novels, *The Portrait of a Lady* (1881), *The Ambassadors* (1903), *The Wings of the Dove* (1902) and *The Golden Bowl* (1904).

From "The American" (1875):

"Upon my word I will think of it," said Valentin. "I will go and listen to Mozart another half hour—I can always think better to music—and profoundly medidate upon it."

The marquis was with his wife when Newman entered their box; he was bland, remote, and correct as usual; or, as it seemed to Newman, even more than usual.

"What do you think of the opera?" he asked our hero. "What do you think of the Don?"

"We all know what Mozart is," said the marquis; "our impressions don't date from this evening. Mozart is youth, freshness, brilliancy, facility—a little too great facility, perhaps. But the execution is here and there deplorably rough."

"I am very curious to see how it ends," said Newman

"You speak as if it were a *feuilleton* in the *Figaro*," observed the marquis. "You have surely seen the opera before."

"Never," said Newman. "I am sure I should have remembered it. Donna Elvira reminds me of Madame de Cinctre; I don't mean in her circumstances, but in the music she sings."

"It is a very nice distinction," laughed the marquis lightly. "There is no great possibility, I imagine, of Madame de Cintre being forsaken."

"Not much!" said Newman. "But what becomes of the Don?"

"The devil comes down—or comes up," said Madame de Bellegarde, "and carries him off. I suppose Zerlina reminds you of me."

"I will go to the *foyer* for a few moments," said the marquis, "and give you a chance to say that the Commander—the man of stone—resembles me." And he passed out of the box.

Nikolai Rimsky-Korsakov

(1844–1908) was born in Tikhvin, Russia, became a naval officer, but by 1865 had already written his first symphony and joined the "Russian Five"—Mussorgsky, Cui, Balakirev and Borodin—as an important nationalist composer. After composing the opera, *The Maid of Pskov* (1872), he resigned from the Navy and became the successful mentor or many young moderns, including Glazunov, Arensky, Liadov and Igor Stravinsky. His best known works include *Scheherazade* (1888). *Capriccio Espagnol* (1887) and the operas *Snow Maiden* (1881), *Sadko* (1896), and *Le Coq d'Or* (1907).

From "Reminiscences of Rimsky-Korsakov" by Y. V. Yastrebtsev:

"I'm not arguing," asserted Rimsky-Korsakov, "Mozart is not Gluck and his *Don Giovanni* is not a minuet, but it by no means has the extraordinary significance that some people once ascribed to it and very likely still do. I don't deny that in *Don Giovanni* a new trend manifested itself (musical characterization and even a certain formlessness in recitative). But this opera was only a first step toward the latest music drama which, despite the fact that it had much in common with its prototype, far outstripped it and, in the persons of Wagner and Glinka, achieved heights unattainable by Mozart."

Then we (Yastrebtsev and Rimsky-Korsakov) exchanged ideas about Mozart's *Don Giovanni*—the delightful duet "La ci darem la mano," Don Giovanni's poetic serenade with its charming mandolin accompaniment, the interesting music expressing

Leporello's fright, and the majestic, even grandiose scene with the Commendatore.

"All this is still new," remarked Rimsky-Korsakov, "almost contemporary."

"Isn't it a fact, though," asked Rimsky-Korsakov, "that Mozart puts constraints on the artist, which hamper and limit his creativity?"

"I don't think," Rimsky-Korsakov concluded, "that even (Richard) Strauss' veneration of Mozart is sincere. It may just be the result of an over-weening egotism. It goes like this—there was the great Mozart; now another genius, superior to Mozart, has appeared, and that is Richard Strauss. Thus, to Strauss, Mozart is simply a stage in the development of German music, the summit of which is now occupied by Strauss himself."

From "My Musical Life" by N. A. Rimsky-Korsakoff, Tudor Publishing Co., New York, 1936:

(In the circle composed of Mussorgski, Balakireff, Cui, and others) Mozart and Haydn were considered out of date and naive; J. S. Bach was held to be petrified . . . Wagner and Rubinstein, sour-sweet; bourgeois Mendelssohn, and dry, childish Mozart.

Having done with our concerts, my wife and I parted with our friends (who stayed in Paris) and left for Russia via Vienna, making brief visits at Lucerne and Zurich and going to see Salzburg with Mozart's house, and the salt mines at Salzkammergut and Konigsee.

Gabriel Urbain Fauré

(1845–1924) spent a great part of his life as an organist, including a long tenure at the Madeleine in Paris, then as teacher and director of the Paris Conservatoire. His *Masques et Bergamasques* (1919) and the *Requiem* (1887) are often performed, as well as many songs.

From a review by Fauré, June 1, 1909:

Mozart's music is particularly difficult to perform. His admirable clarity exacts absolute cleanness; the slightest incorrectness in it stand out like black on white. As I heard Saint-Saens say lately: "It is music in which all the notes must be heard." Essentially simple, natural, it demands a simple, natural expression as well; in other words, that to which its interpreters, even the best intentioned, have least accustomed us.

Ernest Chausson

(1855–1899) was born in Paris, and at age 15 entered the fashionable salon world where he became acquainted with artists and composers. In 1879 Massenet taught him instrumentation; he was influenced also by Cesar Franck. *Poeme* (1896) remains his most notable work though he produced memorable compositions in most traditional forms.

From "Ernest Chausson—the Composer's Life and Works" by Jean-Pierre Barricelli and Leo Weinstein. Univ. of Oklahoma Press, Norman, 1955.

In a letter dated 1889 to Poudaud: "How delightful, how exquisite it ("The Magic Flute") is; you could not ask for anything fresher or more original. It seems to me as if I am reading that score for the first time. A sign of age. As we grow older we have a greater liking for youthfulness. Just take a look at Gounod and see how soft he has grown, artistically speaking. Now he is pressing the score of *Don Juan* to his heart, because he knows that it contains ideas, warmth, life, that is to say things which he does not have or has no longer. Could it be that perchance I too have reached that stage? That would be precociousness. Without flattering myself, I hope to have yet a few years ahead of me. Don't think that I have fallen into writing so-called simple music. No, that is finished for good. That was a delightful moment which could not last. It is not in that direction that we must look. The only thing which is truly ours and which our terrible ancestors have been unable to take away from us is our manner of understanding and feeling. That can always vary with each man. Let us then put as much as possible of ourselves into our works. That is what I am endeavoring to do. And I continue to play without fear and with delight entire acts of the *Flute*.

George Bernard Shaw

(1856–1950), born in Dublin, became the most popular English dramatist of his time. In 1876 he went to London, wrote socialist propaganda and musical reviews and criticism. His first play, *Widowers' Houses*, was produced in 1892 and was followed by a series of brilliant successes, *Arms and the Man* (1894), *Candida* (1894), *Man and Superman* (1903), *John Bull's Other Island* (1904) and *The Doctor's Dilemma* (1906). He received the Nobel Prize in 1925.

From "To a Young Actress—Letters of Bernard Shaw to Molly Tompkins":

I don't know whether you are a musician. If not, you don't know Mozart; and if you don't know Mozart you will never understand my technique. If you are, you must have noticed sometime or another that though a composer may play his music ever so much more beautifully and intelligently than a professional pianist, yet he cannot produce the same effect in a concert room, because he hasn't got the steel in his fingers.

From "Shaw, an Autobiography":

. . . though I began with an extensive knowledge of music, English, German, and Italian, from the sixteenth century to the nineteenth, not by reading books about it but by listening to it and singing it; though I knew the nine symphonies of Beethoven and the three greatest of Mozart's as well as I knew Pop Goes The Weazel; though I had looked at pictures and engravings of pictures until I could recognize the handiwork of the greatest painters at a glance, yet I could not read the Satires of Juvenal in the original Latin, my imprisonment for years in a school where nothing was counted as educational except Latin and Greek having left me unable to read the most conventional Latin epitaph without guessing, or to write a single Ciceronian sentence.

I read Mozart's Succinct Thoroughbass (a scrap of paper with some helpful tips on it which he scrawled for his pupil Sussmaier); and this, many years later, Edward Elgar told me was the only document in existence of the smallest use to a student composer. It was, I grieve to say, of no use to me; but then I was not a young composer . . .

From "Bernard Shaw—Collected Letters 1898–1910" ed. by Dan H. Laurence:

Henley (William Ernest Henley) admired "Cashel Byron"—I have always considered this the mark of a fool, by the way—and among the various literary and artistic Dulcineas whose championship Henley mistook for criticism was Mozart. As I also knew Mozart's value, Henley induced me to write articles on music for his paper the Scots Observer, afterwards the National Observer; and I did write some—not more than half a dozen—perhaps not so many. Henley was an impossible editor. He had no idea of criticism except to glorify the masters he liked, and pursue their rivals with spiteful jealousy. To appreciate Mozart without reviling Wagner was to Henley a black injustice to Mozart.

I have been influenced mainly by works of art in my artificial culture, and have always been more *consciously* susceptible to music and painting than to literature, so that Mozart and Michelangelo count for a great deal in the making of my mind, and that English dramatists after Shakespeare do not count at all . . .

Shaw's music criticism quoted in "Pleasures of Music" ed. by Jacques Barzun, New York, Viking Press, 1951:

. . . every progression in Bach is sanctified by emotion; and Mozart's subtlety, delicacy, and exquisite tender touch and noble feeling were the despair of all the musical world. But Bach's theme was not himself, but his religion; and Mozart was always the dramatist and storyteller, making the men and women of his imagination speak, and dramatizing even the instruments in his orchestra, so that you know their very sex the moment their voices reach you.

. . . (Beethoven's) criticisms, too, become quite consistent and inevitable; for instance, one is no longer tempted to resent his declaration that Mozart wrote nothing worth considering but parts of *Die Zauberflote* (those parts, perhaps, in which the beat of "*dein sanfter Flugel*" is heard), and to retort upon him by silly comparisons of his tunes with "*Non piu andrai*" and "*Deh vieni alla finestra*." The man who wrote the Eighth Symphony has a right to rebuke the man who put his raptures of elation, tenderness, and nobility into the mouths of a drunken libertine, a silly peasant girl, and a conventional fine lady, instead of confining them to himself, glorying in them, and uttering them without motley as the univeral inheritance.

From "The Great Composers" by Bernard Shaw, ed. by Louis Crompton:

Mozart, (Beethoven's) greatest predecessor in his own department, had from his childhood been washed, combed, splendidly dressed, and beautifully behaved in the presence of royal personages and peers. His childish outburst at the Pompadour, "Who is this woman who does not kiss me? The Queen kisses me," would be incredible of Beethoven, who was still an unlicked cub even when he had grown into a very grizzly bear. Mozart had the refinement of convention and society as well as the refinement of nature and of the solitudes of the soul. Mozart and Gluck are refined as the court of Louis XIV was refined: compared to them socially Beethoven was an obstreperous Bohemian: a man of the people. Haydn, so superior to envy that he declared his junior, Mozart, to be the greatest composer that ever lived, could not stand Beethoven: Mozart, more far seeing, listened to his playing, and said "You will hear of him some day;" but the two would never have hit it off together had Mozart lived long enough to try. Beethoven had a moral horror of Mozart, who in Don Giovanni had thrown a halo of enchantment round an aristocratic blackguard, and then, with the unscrupulous moral versatility of a born dramatist, turned round to cast a halo of divinity round Sarastro, setting his words to the only music yet written that would not sound out of place in the mouth of God.

For my own part, if I do not care to rhapsodize much about Mozart, it is because I am so violently prepossessed in his favor that I am capable of supplying any possible deficiency in his work by my imagination. Gounod has devoutly declared that Don Giovanni has been to him all his life a revelation of perfection, a miracle, a work without fault. I smile indulgently at Gounod, since I cannot afford to give myself away so generously (there being, no doubt, less of me); but I am afraid my fundamental attitude towards Mozart is the same as his. In my small-boyhood I by good luck had an opportunity of learning the Don thoroughly, and if it were only for the sense of the value of fine workmanship which I gained from it, I should still esteem that lesson the most important part of my education. Indeed, it educated me artistically in all sorts of ways, and disqualified me only in one—that of criticizing Mozart fairly. Everyone appears a sentimental, hysterical bungler in comparison when anything brings his finest work vividly back to me.

Sir Edward Elgar

(1857–1934) was born in Broadheath, England, son of a musician, and early learned to play in a local orchestra, though he did not begin composing until mid-life, when his work almost immediately met with acceptance. His *Enigma Variations* (1899), *Cockaigne* (In London Town) (1901), and symphonies, *Cello Concerto* (1919) are standard items in the repertory, to say nothing of the *Pomp and Circumstance* marches *de riguer* at every high school commencement.

From "Letters of Edward Elgar" Geoffrey Bles, London, 1956:

to 'My dear Chignell,' January 1901
Here are two little things of Mozart for organ & strings (Sonatas K.67–69). I want you to play 'em at the Phil Concert. They were written for Salzburg where the organ was a real South German duffer; but the music is delightful & I think you can make a 'pretty effect'—you will see the spirit of the things is quite different to the austere North-German-Bach organ style; we'll talk over the stops sometime.

From "Edward Elgar, His Life & Music" by Diana M. McVeagh:

I (Elgar) once ruled a score for the same instruments with the same number of bars as Mozart's G minor Symphony, and in that framework I wrote a symphony, following as far as possible the same outlines for his themes and the same modulations. I did this on my own initiative as I was groping in the dark after light, but looking back after thirty years, I don't know any discipline from which I learnt so much.

VIVA MOZART

From "Edward Elgar, a Creative Life" by Jerrold Northrop Moore, Oxford University Press, New York, 1984:

I (Elgar) seem to remember Mozart was asked to play from Vivaldi's concertos—invent an upper part to Vivaldi's figured bass.... I always like to think we own the very book that the Wonder Child played from!

Mozart is the musician from whom everyone should learn form.

From "An Elgar Companion" Edited by Christopher Redwood, Sequoia Publishing Co., Ashborre, Derbyshire:

Mozart and Beethoven were his (Elgar, Senior's) 'dearly beloved' composers, and as his son Edward points to a portrait of Mozart on the wall of his study, he remarks, "That is my man." Thus the boy entered the world and was nurtured in a rarified atmosphere of music.

The Mozart tradition lingered in the Elgar household, for Elgar's father had been a pupil of Sutton of Dover, and Sutton had been a pupil of Michael Kelly, and Michael Kelly, the Dublin boy who became a famous operatic singer and composer, was the intimate friend of Mozart.

"Mozart is rarely or never, played today as he was in my boyhood," says Sir Edward. "Nowadays the players play either too rigidly or with sentimentality. The tradition seems to be dead.

Giacomo Puccini

(1858–1924), a native of Lucca, Italy, descended from a musical family, and at the Milan Conservatory studied under Ponchielli who inspired him to write opera. With *Manon Lescaut* (1893), *La Boheme* (1896) and *Tosca* (1900) he was universally acclaimed as Verdi's successor in Italian opera. He wrote for the Metropolitan Opera *The Girl of the Golden West* (1910). His most popular opera, after *La Boheme*, is probably *Madame Butterfly* (1904).

From "Immortal Bohemian" by Dante del Fiorentino:

Asked how he could compose immortal operas in a filthy club, "It's like this," Giacomo explained. "Mozart once lived in a house crammed with musicians. There was a particularly noisy violinist on the floor above him, and a singing teacher next door. When Mozart was asked how he could live in such a bedlam, he replied: 'The noise is necessary for composition, because it gives me new ideas.' Personally I agree with Mozart."

Gustav Mahler

(1860–1911) was born in Kalischt, Bohemia, studied at the Vienna Conservatory, and at age 25 became conductor of the Prague Opera, the first of many conducting positions that included the Opera orchestras of Budapest, Hamburg, Vienna and the New York Metropolitan as well as the New York Philharmonic (1909–1911). Author of nine symphonies and song cycles *Kindertotenlieder* (1904) and *Das Lied von der Erde* (1910), his works have achieved great popularity and are regularly scheduled in concert halls throughout the world.

VIVA MOZART

From "Gustav Mahler" by Alma Mahler, ed. by Donald Mitchell:

Rodin fell in love with his model (Mahler); he was really unhappy when we (Mahler and his wife) had to leave Paris, for he wanted to work on the bust much longer. His method was unlike that of any other sculptor I have had the opportunity of watching. He first made flat surfaces in the rough lump, and then added little pellets of clay which he rolled between his fingers while he talked. He worked by adding to the lump instead of subtracting from it. As soon as we left he smoothed it all down and next day added more. I scarcely ever saw him with a tool in his hand. He said Mahler's head was a mixture of Franklin's, Frederick the Great's and Mozart's. After Mahler's death, Rodin showed me a head in marble, which he had done from memory, and pointed out how like it was. A custodian of the Rodin Museum in Paris actually labelled it 'Mozart'.

He had difficulty in breathing and was given oxygen (as he lay dying). Then uremia—and the end. . . . Mahler lay with dazed eyes; one finger was conducting on the quilt. There was a smile on his lips and twice he said: 'Mozart!'

I still remember a talk we had about Mozart during a sledge-drive. Mahler talking a lot about 'Constanzerl,' whose speedy remarriage he could not forgive, and about Mozart's wretched life. He loved him as a human being more than anyone who ever lived.

From "Recollections of Gustav Mahler" by Natalie Bauer-Lechner:

... the next work to engage Mahler's attention in Vienna was *The Magic Flute*. In the course of the first rehearsal of the opera, a delicate cello passage continued to sound far too loud, in spite of his repeated exhortations. He suddenly realized, to his amazement, that he was surrounded by an orchestra large enough for a Wagner opera. This had been customary here, year in and year out, and the fine bloom that lies on the work had naturally been worn away. Mahler at once sent half the orchestra home, whereupon they applauded him and cried 'Bravo!' 'I see I am a success!' he exclaimed laughingly, 'But don't think I am doing this as a favor. On the contrary, I am convinced that such a big orchestra destroys the fragrance and the magic of a work by Mozart.'

After an enchanting new rendering of *Zar and Zimmermann*, *The Magic Flute* is now being largely restaged. Mahler told me that he wanted to bring out its fairy-tale quality as far as possible. For example, he intended to treat the flute aria of Tamino like the Orpheus and Arion legends, with every conceivable animal wandering up to listen. And a few days later, coming from rehearsal, he told me: 'My animals are marvellous! I have shown all the extras what they have to do. It will really be quaint and amusing. First a lion appears, followed by his mate, and they lie down affectionately beside each other. Then a tiger peeps out from behind a bush and slinks slowly forward, ears alert. Birds come flying up; a hare lopes by, pricks up its ears (how I manage that is my secret!) and listens. Then a giant snake slithers up, and, to top it off, a crocodile flops out of the Nile. You can imagine the naive effect when, after all this, Tamino complains that everybody is coming except his Pamina. But the moment Papageno's piccolo sounds, the whole company takes to its heels. I hope people will understand it, and not take it as an insult to their "classical" Mozart!

(Mahler said) there are really not more than three perfect German opera composers: Mozart, whose sureness of aim in all that he did is unparalleled, Wagner—and you'd be surprised at the third.... Lortzing.... That's not to speak of Beethoven and his unique *Fidelio*, which is *hors concours*. For wherever he reached out his hand, the greatest art arose!

IGNACE JAN PADEREWSKI

(1860–1941), born in Kurylowka, Poland, was celebrated principally as a great pianist, but he was politically active and served as Premier of the first Polish Republic, later as President of the Polish Government in Exile during World War II. His compositions for the piano, orchestra and chamber ensembles are all eclipsed by his famous *Minuet in G* (1887).

From "Paderewski" by Charlotte Kellogg:

We find him (Paderewski) now in Warsaw, writing a piece that remains the most popular of all he wrote, the Minuet in G, and the account of how he happened to write it is one of the amusing stories he was asked to tell many times. When he arrived in Warsaw he found there the doctor who had been so kind to him in Zakopane; and often with the old man was an elderly friend, who was as fond of Mozart as the doctor was. If Paderewski dropped in of an evening, from the Kerntopf's, the two at once asked him to play again familiar Mozart scores. They wished nothing else—above all, no music of modern composers . . .

As he invariably did, Paderewski thought of an amusing way to end a tiresome situation. He would write something in Mozart's manner, play it as if it were Mozart's own, and see what happened. As was his habit, he told no one of this plan but wrote the now famous Minuet. Soon he was playing it and watching the two old gentlemen out of the corner of his eye. They were delighted with the unfamiliar Mozart composition and asked him to play it again.

"But why have you not played this before?" they cried.

"Because I myself have just written it," he replied solemnly.

At first they refused to believe him, and then seemed confused, angry, so mixed up in their minds about it that he was a bit ashamed of his successful joke. However, once the elderly gentlemen recovered, they did not resent it; nor has the world since!

Edward Alexander MacDowell

(1861–1908) was born in New York City, but at age 15 was taken to Paris and spent the next fourteen years studying and teaching piano in Europe. At 35 he became Professor of Music at Columbia University. His health and mental faculties declined after 1905, and he died insane at age 47. His two piano concertos are infrequently played, but his *Woodland Sketches* (1888) often hold the concert platform.

From "Critical and Historical Essays" by E. Macdowell:

. . . If we read on one page of some history (every history of music has such a page) that Mozart's sonatas are sublime, that they do not contain one note of mere filigree work, and that they far transcend anything written for the harpsichord or clavichord by Haydn or his contemporaries, we echo that saying, and, if necessary, quote the "authorities." Now if one had occasion to read over some of the clavichord music of the period, possibly it might seem strange that Mozart's sonatas did not impress with their magnificence. One might even harbor a lurking doubt as to the value of the many seemingly bare runs and unmeaning passages. Then one would probably turn back to the authorities for an explanation and find perhaps the following: "The inexpressible charm of Mozart's music leads us to forget the marvellous learning bestowed upon its construction. Later composers have sought to conceal the constructional points of the sonata which Mozart never cared to disguise, so that incautious students have sometimes failed to discern in them the veritable 'pillars of the house,' and have accused Mozart of poverty of style because he left them boldly exposed to view, as a great architect delights to expose the piers upon which the tower of his cathedral depends for its support." (Rockstro, *History of Music*, p. 269). Now this is all very fine, but it is nonsense, for Mozart's sonatas are anything but cathedrals. It is time to cast aside this shibboleth of printer's ink and paper and look the thing itself straight in the face. It is a fact that Mozart's sonatas are compositions entirely unworthy of the author of the *Magic Flute*, or of any composer with pretensions to anything beyond mediocrity. They are written in a style of flashy harpsichord virtuosity such as Liszt never descended to, even in those of his works at which so many persons are accustomed to sneer.

Frederic Delius

(1862–1934) was born in Bradford, England of German parentage. Destined for a career in business, he left England in protest, spent some years in Florida as a fruit grower, studying music in his spare time and finally returning to France as a teacher and composer. His works, songs, orchestral and choral, are slight yet enjoy a *success de estime* in many quarters.

AND
Percy Grainger

(1882–1961) was born in Melbourne, Australia, studied piano with his mother, and in 1901 settled as a concert pianist in London. A friend of Delius and Grieg, he began composing music based on folk songs. He moved to the United States in 1914 and spent the rest of his life principally here. He is known best for small pieces, *Mock Morris* (1910) and *Country Gardens* (1919).

(Percy Grainger comments): Both of us worshipped Walt Whitman, Wagner, Grieg and Jens Peter Jacobsen. Both of us detested the music of the Haydn-Mozart-Beethoven period. 'If a man tells me he likes Mozart, I know in advance that he is a bad musician,' Delius was fond of saying.*

RICHARD STRAUSS

(1864–1949) (unrelated to Johann Strauss of waltz fame) was born in Garmisch-Partenkirchen, Bavaria, the son of a lead horn player in the Munich Opera orchestra who recognized the boy's talent and brought him up on the great classics. At 21 he began a career of conductorship and composition. He is regarded as one of the great Romantic moderns, outstanding for such popular operas as *Salome* (1905), *Elektra* (1909), and *Der Rosenkavalier* (1911) and the tone poems *Don Juan* (1888), *Death and Transfiguration* (1888) and *Ein Heldenleben* (1897) etc., and many songs.

From "Composers on Music" edited by Sam Morgenstern:

Whence stem the indescribable melodies of our classicists (Haydn, Mozart, Beethoven, Schubert), for which no models exist? Even in Johann Sebastian

*From *Frederic Delius* by Peter Warlock.

Bach's Adagios and in the works of his son, Philipp Emanuel, we hardly find themes which can be compared with the soaring, endless melodies of Mozart—not only in the arias of his dramatic works, but also in his instrumental works (I am thinking particularly of his *G minor String Quintet*). What then is direct inspiration, primary invention, and what is the work of the intelligence in these divine forms? Where is the boundary between intellectual activity and imagination?

The question is especially difficult to decide among our classicists; the wealth of their melodies is so enormous, the melody itself so new, so original and at the same time so individually varied, that it is difficult to determine the line between the first immediate inspiration and its continuation, its extension to the finished, expanded singing phrase. Particularly in Mozart and Schubert who died so young, and at the same time created a lifework of such colossal scope! (My father always said: "What Mozart did, that is, composed up to his thirty-sixth year, the best copyist of today could not write down in the same amount of time.") It must have been prompted—as in the lovely concluding tableau in the first act of Pfitzner's *Palestrina*—by the flying pen of angels. For the kind of work which is to be seen in Beethoven's sketchbooks can hardly exist here. Here everything seems immediate inspiration.

It has become the custom to treat this most sublime of all tonal masters (Mozart) as a "rococo artist," to represent his work as the epitome of the ornamental and the playful. Though it is correct to say that he was one who solved all "problems" before they were even posed, that in him passion is divested of everything earthly and seems to be viewed from a bird's-eye perspective, it is equally true that his work contains—even when transfigured, spiritualized and liberated from reality—all phases of human experience from the monumental, dark grandeur of the Commandant's scene in *Don Giovanni* to the daintiness of the Zerlina arias, the heavenly frivolities of *Figaro*, and the deliberate ironies of *Cosi fan tutte*.

With less amplitude, but with no less abundance the entire gamut of human feeling is expressed in his non-dramatic creations. To set up a uniform Mozart style for the reproduction of this infinitely fine and richly organized soul-picture is as foolish as it is superficial.

In Susanna's garden aria, in Belmonte's and Ferrando's A major and Octavio's G major arias, Eros himself sings in Mozart's melody; Love in its most beautiful, purest forms speaks to our feelings. Zerlina's two arias are not merely the expression of an ordinary, betrayed peasant girl. In the slow section of Donna Anna's so-called "Letter" aria, in both arias of the Countess in *Figaro*, we have before us the creations of the Ideal, which I can only compare with Plato's "Ideas," the prototypes of visions projected into real life. Almost immediately on Bach follows the miracle of Mozart, with his perfection and absolute idealization of the melody of human song—I might call it the Platonic Idea or Prototype—not to be recognized by the eye, not to be grasped by the understanding, but to be divined by consciousness as most godly, which the ear is permitted to "breathe in." Mozartian melody is detached from every earthly form—the "thing in itself," like Plato's Eros, poised between heaven and earth, between the mortal and the immortal—liberated from the "will," of the unconscious, into the final mysteries, into the realm of the "archetypes."

From "Richard Strauss" by Norman Del Mar:

Certainly to occupy himself directly with the music of Mozart was for Strauss a major incentive, for his was no superficial devotion. He was once asked to write a preface for a book on 'Mozart and Munich' but actually replied, 'I cannot write about Mozart, I can only worship him.' Towards the end of his life he even dedicated a work to the 'spirit of the divine Mozart.' He took every opportunity when conducting to include a Mozart symphony in his programmes, and in the great E flat and G minor Symphonies was in the habit of returning a second time to the Trios after the *Menuetto da capo* because 'such music should be heard more than once.'

(letter to Stefan Zweig) Your letter . . . drives me to despair! This Jewish obstinacy! It drives one into antisemitism! This racial pride, this feeling of solidarity—even I feel a difference. Do you imagine I have ever been led in the course of a single action by the thought that I am Germanic (perhaps, qui le said)? Do you suppose that Mozart was consciously 'Aryan' in his composing? For me there are only two sorts of people; those who have talent and those who haven't . . .

(Walking in Salzburg with the producer Rudolf Hartmann) Strauss said, 'Come on, let's go round by my beloved Mozart.'

(from a letter to Hugo Burghauser, October 1946) . . . I am even busy with an idea for a double concerto for clarinet and bassoon thinking especially of your beautiful tone—nevertheless apart from a few sketched out themes it still remains no more than an intention . . . Perhaps it would interest you; my father always used to say 'It was Mozart who wrote most beautifully for the bassoon.' But then he was also the one to have all the most beautiful thoughts, coming straight from down from the skies!

JEAN SIBELIUS

(1865–1957), born in Tavastehus, Finland, studied law at the University of Helsinki but soon switched to the Conservatory where he distinguished himself so promptly that the Government gave him a grant to study abroad. At 28 he received a lifetime pension and thenceforth produced a succession of great works: seven symphonies, ten tone poems—one of them, *Finlandia* (1899), now regarded virtually as his country's national anthem. He, along with Richard Strauss and Igor Stravinsky, were considered the great "three S's" of their era, rivalling the "three B's" (Bach, Beethoven and Brahms) of an earlier time.

From "Jean Sibelius" by Karl Ekman, translated by Edward Birse:

I played chamber music as often as I had a chance (when a young man) and the repertory included my own compositions. My usual fellow-musicians were Theodore Spiering, later a conductor in America, Klingenberg, the pianist, and Fini Henriques, the Danish composer, who remains a close friend of mine to this day. Henriques had in his qualifications and adaptiveness all that I lacked. I thought I discerned something quite uncommon in him, he seemed to me to be a new Mozart.

from a letter dated October 25, 1890, Vienna, to Martin Wegelius (quoted in the above book):

Vienna lived entirely in music. The power of the musical traditions was great. The air was full of memories, not only of Schubert's and Beethoven's days, but also of Mozart's time. Among the oral traditions about Mozart I remember it being said that he could never get the overture to *The Marriage of Figaro* played fast enough: it should have been played *prestissimo*.

From "The Music of Jean Sibelius" by Burnett James:

Perhaps because of his early ambitions, never entirely crushed, to become a concert violinist, Sibelius always wrote particularly well for strings. But his scoring all through is remarkably distinctive and relevant to his orchestral thinking. He considered Mozart and Mendelssohn to have been the greatest masters of the orchestra, meaning thereby that when writing for the orchestra they, unlike masters of the piano, conceived it as a whole and thought clearly in terms of orchestral texture.

Ferrucio Benenuto Busoni

(1866–1924), born in Florence, was taught music by his parents almost exclusively and made his Vienna debut as a pianist at age 9. Later he became a well known teacher and arranger for the piano, instructing throughout Europe. His principal works are the operas *Arlecchino* (1917) and *Doctor Faust* (1925), the latter left unfinished at his death.

From "The Sackbut" Curwen & Sons, 1921 and quoted in "Mozart in Retrospect" by A. Hyatt King:

This is how I think of Mozart: he is up to the present the most perfect manifestation of musical talent.

The pure musician looks up to him disarmed and content.

His short life and fecundity enhance his perfection to the point of the phenomenal.

The untroubled beauty of his work irritates.

His sense of form is almost superhuman. Like a masterpiece of sculpture, his art, viewed from any side, is a perfect picture.

He has the instinct of the animal to adapt his task to the uttermost limit, but not beyond that of his powers.

He does not attempt anything rash.

He finds without seeking and seeks not what is undiscoverable, that is to say perhaps rather undiscoverable for him.

He possessed an unusual wealth of material but never exhausts it.

He can express a great diversity of things, but never attempts to utter too many at once.

He is passionate, but preserves chivalrous form.

He bears all characters in himself, but only as their exponent.

With the riddle he provides the solution.

His standards are astonishingly true, but they can be measured and defined.

He disposes of light and shadow, but his light does not pain, and his darkness shows a clear outline.

He has a witticism ready to meet any situation, even the most tragic; in the merriest he can present a solemn mein.

He is universal through his adroitness.

He can draw upon any glass because he never drinks one to the dregs.

He stands so high that he sees further than all, and therefore sees everything on rather a small scale.

His palace is immeasurably great, but he never steps outside the walls.

Through the windows of it he sees Nature. The window frame is also the frame of nature.

Gladness is his predominant feature. He covers even the most unpleasant things with a smile.

His is not the smile of a diplomat or an actor, but of a pure mind, yet that of a man of the world.

His mind is not pure through lack of knowledge.

He has not remained simple and has not become *raffine*.

He has a temperament but not a nervous one, he is an idealist but not unmaterial: a realist without unpleasantness.

He is a burgher as well as an aristocrat, but never a peasant or a rebel.

He is a friend of order: miracles and devilries preserve with him their 16 and 32 bars.

He is religious as far as religion is identical with harmony.

In him the antique and the rococo are combined to perfection, though without resulting in a new architecture.

Architecture is the art most akin to his.

He is the prime and round number, the sum total, a conclusion and not a beginning.

He is as youthful as an adolescent and wise as an old man—never out of date and never modern: carried to the grave and yet ever alive. His very human smile transfigured still beams upon us.

ROMAIN ROLLAND

(1866–1944) was born in Clamecy, France, son of a lawyer. He early showed great musical aptitude and began a lifelong dedication to writing about music and musicians, eventually directing the study of musical history at the Sorbonne. In 1904 he published his masterpiece, the enormous novel about a musician, *Jean-Christophe* which established him as one of France's foremost authors. He also published biographies of Beethoven, Handel, Michelangelo and others and was awarded the Nobel Prize for Literature in 1915.

From "Some Musicians of Former Days" by Romain Rolland, translated by Mary Blaiklock:

(Mozart) was able to do what he wished (in music), and he never wished to do what was beyond him. His work is like a sweet scent in his life—perhaps like a beautiful flower whose only care is to live. So easy was creation to him that at times it poured from him in a double or triple stream, and he performed incredible feats of mental activity without thinking about them. He would compose a prelude while writing a fugue; and once when he played a sonata for pianoforte and violin at a concert, he composed it the day before, between eleven o'clock and midnight, hurriedly writing the violin part, and having no time to write down the piano part or to rehearse it with his partner. The next day he played from memory what he had composed in his head (April 8, 1781).

Mozart knew sadness in every form; he knew the pangs of mental suffering, the dread of the unknown, and the sadness of a lonely soul. . . . Sometimes Mozart's individual self and his inner god engage in sublime discourse, especially at times when his dejected spirit seeks a refuge from the world. This duality of spirit may be often seen in Beethoven's works; though Beethoven's soul was violent, capricious, passionate and strange. Mozart's soul, on the other hand, is youthful and gentle, suffering at times from an excess of affection yet full of peace; and he sings his troubles in rhythmical phrases, in his own charming way, and ends by falling asleep in the midst of his tears with a smile on his face.

ARNOLD BENNETT

(1867–1931) was born in Staffordshire, England, studied art and law but at age 21 went to London to become editor of a woman's magazine. He tried his hand at fiction and was an overnight success with *The Grand Babylon Hotel* (1902). He was a prolific author of criticism, fiction and drama and became one of the 'big three' English novelists of the 1920's along with H. G. Wells and John Galsworthy. His best known work is *The Old Wives' Tale* (1908).

From "The Journal of Arnold Bennett":

Friday, July 27th, 1917. London, Yacht Club.
Dined at flat and then with M. to *Marriage of Figaro*. Dramatically the last act is very poor in both scenes. Musically it is as good as the rest. Shaw grumbled much at the performance. The sentimental interest, as Newman said to me, is the best part of the opera, and the Figaro music is not very surpassing. The sentimental songs were celestial.

Thursday, October 27th, 1927.
I went to South Kensington Museum to think, and I thought. Then I wrote the penultimate section of my story "The Wind" in about an hour. I dined with

Geoffrey Russell at the Reform, and we went to the Lener concert together at Queen's Hall. All Mozart. I thought that exclusive Mozart would be trying, but it wasn't.

MARCEL PROUST

(1871–1922) was born in Auteuil. outside of Paris. A frail child, he was a semi-invalid who attended schools irregularly but at 18 enrolled in a sedentary branch of the army, and after 1890 entered the Sorbonne to study law; however, he was interested in the social life of the artistocracy and spent the next few years as a Parisian 'man about town.' After the death of his parents in 1906 he became a virtual recluse in a cork-lined room at 102 Boulevard Haussmann suffering from asthma, and settled down to write his masterpiece *Remembrance of Things Past*, the first part of which appeared in *1913*.

From "Swann in Love" section of "Remembrance of Things Past":

Mme de Gallardon drew herself up and, putting on an even chillier expression, though still apparently concerned about the Prince's health, said to her cousin:

"Oriane" (at once Mme des Laumes looked with amused astonishment towards an invisible third person, whom she seemed to call to witness that she had never authorised Mme de Gallardon to use her Christian name), "I should be pleased if you would look in for a moment tomorrow evening to hear a clarinet quartet by Mozart. I should like to have your opinion of it."

She seemed not to much to be issuing an invitation as to be asking a favour, and to want the Princess's opinion of the Mozart quintet just as though it had been a dish invented by a new cook, whose talent it was most important that an epicure should come to judge.

"But I know that quintet quite well. I can tell you now—that I adore it."

Gustav Holst

(1874–1934) was born in Cheltenham, England. A student at the Royal College of Music, he became trombonist and organist, beginning a lifetime of teaching and composing orchestral and choral pieces as well as songs and piano works, culminating in the orchestral suite *The Planets* (1917), his most often played long work today.

Quoted in "The Heritage of Music" by Gustav Holst:

Purcell's most famous opera *Dido and Aeneas* was written about the year 1689, and not nine years before, as was previously thought. Even so, it is one of the most original expressions of genius in all opera. Mozart remains the greatest prodigy in musical history, but he was brought up in a fine tradition—in opera, as well as other music.

From: "Gustav Holst" by Imogen Holst:

Nor had he (Holst) any patience with 'freedom for

freedom's sake.' 'We know now,' he wrote, 'that freedom is something to be acquired by rigid training and severe struggle, unless you happen to be one of the true aristocrats, like Mozart, in whom artistic self-control is born.'

Arnold Schoenberg

(1874–1951) was born in Vienna and became an American citizen after the Nazi persecution of the Jews, having already made a name for himself in Berlin as the developer of the twelve-tone system adopted by some modern composers, notably Webern and Berg. His best known works are the tone poems *Pelleas and Melisande* (1902) and *Transfigured Night* (1943) and his *Violin Concerto* (1936) and *Piano Concerto* (1942).

From "Schoenberg Remembered" by Dika Newlin:

Schoenberg once said that Mozart once presented to a pianist one very low note, one very high note, and two in the middle register, and asked him to play them all at once. Of course, the answer was that the pianist played the two middle notes with his nose! Schoenberg tried to demonstrate this at the piano—amid howls of laughter in which I joined—and finally admitted, "This man must have had a longer nose than I!"

He (Schoenberg) is still talking about last Saturday's performance of *Figaro* which I was so lucky as to listen to (in part) by his side. He says he wishes every one of us had heard it, not so much for the execution (which was poor) as for the marvelous qualities of the music. Its most especial merit, according to him, is its explosive character, which makes it so dramatic. This is produced by the juxtaposition, within one fairly large section, of a great many smaller ideas which contrast violently with one another.

His (Schoenberg's) cutest remark of the day was made in Structural Functions (where we analyzed Mozart's C-minor Fantasia), in reply to a student who told him that the reason all the people of last year's analysis class didn't have Mozart sonatas was that he'd told half the class to buy Mozart and half Schubert. "Yes. Quite so!" the master replied. "One half of each student buys Mozart and the other half buys Schubert. This is what I meant!"

I'd hoped to get Uncle Arnold to look some more at my thesis today—but no . . . He did, though, analyze things which had a direct application to what I am doing: Brahms' G Minor Piano Quartet and Mozart's G Minor String Quintet. We had a funny experience with that last one: I was peaceably playing the upper parts on my piano, and Mr. Stein the lower ones on his, when suddenly I became aware of an echo of my part from the other piano! I suspected what was going on, but didn't say anything until afterwards, when I was alone with Mr. Stein. Yes, sure enough, the old man had been banging out that melody right along with (or a little behind) me. He loves it so, he couldn't help it!

Uncle Arnold looked at what I'd done with my Minuet of my *Serenade*; has many suggestions, and showed many examples of Mozart's finesse in Minuets. "This should be a stimulation to you," says he to me, and then, turning to the rest of the class, "even to the rest of you who will not be composers!"

He (Schoenberg) rushed over to the bookcase, fetched down his copy of the Mozart symphonies, and started to talk at length about their orchestration. No point was too small to spend at least five minutes on: why the viola appeared above the second violin (I think he found at least three good reasons for this, and gave a full justification of each one of them!), or why two horns instead of one, were used in such-and-such a place. Everything he could possibly talk about, in short, he talked about. When he ran out of subjects for commentary, he began to sing, ostensibly to demonstrate the wonderful character of Mozart's melodies!

From "Schoenberg and the God Idea" by Pamela C. White:

My (Schoenberg's) teachers were primarily Bach and Mozart, and secondarily Beethoven, Brahms and Wagner. . . . From Mozart I learned:
 1. Inequality of phrase-length.
 2. Co-ordination of heterogeneous characters to form a thematic unity.
 3. Deviation from even-number construction in the theme and its component parts.
 4. The art of forming subsidiary ideas.
 5. The art of introduction and transition.

VIVA MOZART

CHARLES IVES

(1874–1954) was born in Danbury, Connecticut, son of a music teacher and conductor. He studied music at Yale and divided his career between music and composition and business. He founded a successful insurance company and for the latter part of his life wrote little music. His *Symphony No. 3* (1911) won a Pulitzer Prize in 1947 and today his 'advanced' works are finding wider audiences.

From "Charles E. Ives Memos" edited by John Kirkpatick:

"Reber (———) had his good points. He had a beautiful tone on the strings, and played Mozart perfectly. I'll have to admit I enjoyed playing Mozart with him, but a whole afternoon of Mozart is a whole afternoon of Mozart (I was going to say something worse, which I occasionally know how to do)."

"Hasn't music always been too much an emasculated art? Mozart etc. helped."*

---

*Note by Kirkpatick: Ives's reaction to Mozart would very well be explained by the kind of Mozart performance that was fashionable when Ives was a young man—smooth and daintily smirking like Dresden china figurines. The Wagner cult had belittled all earlier music except Beethoven, but the twentieth century has found Mozart's music far more masculine than Wagner's.

Albert Schweitzer

(1875–1965), the great humanitarian, was born in Kaysersberg, Alsace, son of a vicar, and studied organ as a young man, becoming organist for the Bach Strasbourg concerts for several years. But he combined his musical bent with a devotion to medicine and received an M.D. degree from Strasbourg University while teaching music there. He spent much of his subsequent life on medical missions to Africa, and was awarded the Nobel Peace Prize in 1952.

From "Music in the Life of Albert Schweitzer" by Charles R. Joy:

Bach was a poet; but he lacked the gift of expression. His language was without distinction, and his poetic taste was no more developed than that of his contemporaries. Would he otherwise have accepted so gladly the libretti of Picander?

Nonetheless, he was a poet in his soul, in that he looked in a text first of all for the poetry it contained. What a difference there was between him and Mozart! Mozart is purely a musician; he takes a given text and clothes it in a beautiful melody.

Doctor ——— Ehlers used to spend a little time (with Doctor Schweitzer) each summer . . . She says "Though the room in which I used to practise was next to his study, it never disturbed the Doctor to hear me practise; he admitted he missed it when I stopped. Often he would come in, sit down, listen to my playing, make his remarks about the music, and sometimes ask for one of his favorite pieces.

When I played the piano, he almost always asked for Mozart; he loves Mozart.

Pierre Monteux

(1875–1964) was born in Paris, started studying the violin at age 4, and at 9 entered the Paris Conservatoire. At 12 he conducted a Parisian orchestra, the activity that was to become his lifelong career. Among his many premieres were Schoenberg's *Pelleas et Melisande*, Stravinsky's *Petrushka* and *The Rite of Spring*. He was naturalized as an American citizen in 1942 and was conductor for many years of the Boston and San Francisco Symphony Orchestras.

From "It's All in the Music" by Doris Monteux:

quoting Monteux, "I hope you understand me, but it is my feeling that music interpretation has become 'too slick' and too much stress is on technique and too little on taste, and on understanding the partition (score). Yes, that is it. There is a lack of taste in the young musician of today. I felt it recently when a young pianist who had been praised by critics for his interpretation of Bartok played a concert of Mozart with me. The fingers played the notes, but Mozart with his charming moments, his *esprit* and adorable *espieglerie*, his youthful romanticism, were simply not there. I felt, 'What a dull fellow this is.' What a pity!"

Bruno Walter

(1876–1962) was born in Berlin and educated at the Stern Conservatory, Berlin. He became one of the most celebrated conductors of his day, leading the opera orchestras of Vienna, Munich, Berlin, Leipzig, London and New York. He was guest conductor of the New York Philharmonic, the San Francisco Symphony and many of the large orchestras in the United States.

From "Of Music and Music Making" by Bruno Walter:

On the occasion of January 27, 1956: The thought of the imminent celebration of the bicentenary of Mozart's birth has brought home to me my obligation to acknowledge, for once in writing, the genius whom, as a musician, I have endeavored to serve all my life. Above all, this must be an expression of gratitude for the sublime happiness with which the creativeness of Mozart has illumined, has blessed, my life. . . .

I am . . . aware of only one personal statement of Mozart's that points towards those depths of his soul which are witnessed by his music. This exception to the usually so worldy tone of his numerous letters is contained in a communication of the thirty-one-year-old Mozart to his father:

> 'As death is, strictly speaking, the true end and aim of our lives, I have for the last few years made myself so well acquainted with this true, best friend of mankind that his image no longer terrifies, but calms and consoles me. And I

thank God for giving me the opportunity of learning to look upon death as the key which unlocks the gate of true bliss. I never lie down to rest without thinking that, young as I am, before the dawn of another day I may be no more; and yet nobody who knows me would call me morose and discontented. For this blessing I thank my creator every day, and wish from my heart that I could share it with all my fellowmen.'

So he thought of death every day, 'in blissfulness;' this fully shows how close to eternity his heart was; it shows the unearthly harmony in it which informs his music as a seraphic sound. For the rest, however, this most communicative, not to say, talkative, of men was silent about those depths of his soul of which he himself may for long periods of time have been only vaguely conscious. Only the *Magic Flute* unsealed his lips, and there he laid bare his heart— in Sarastro's and Tamino's words and strains; and in the former's pronouncements, the world should recognize Mozart's own spiritual testament. Yet though Tamino's striving was glorously crowned in the end, Mozart was glorified only *sub specie aeterni*— long after his troubled earthly life had found its sad end. Yet even in this wearisome earthly pilgrimage we may discern a wondrous analogy with the errand of his hero in the *Magic Flute*. As to Tamino, the 'good gods' had granted to Mozart the protection of sound against the dangers besetting his path: the music that accompanied him on his life's journey gave him the courage, the noble serenity, and the

VIVA MOZART

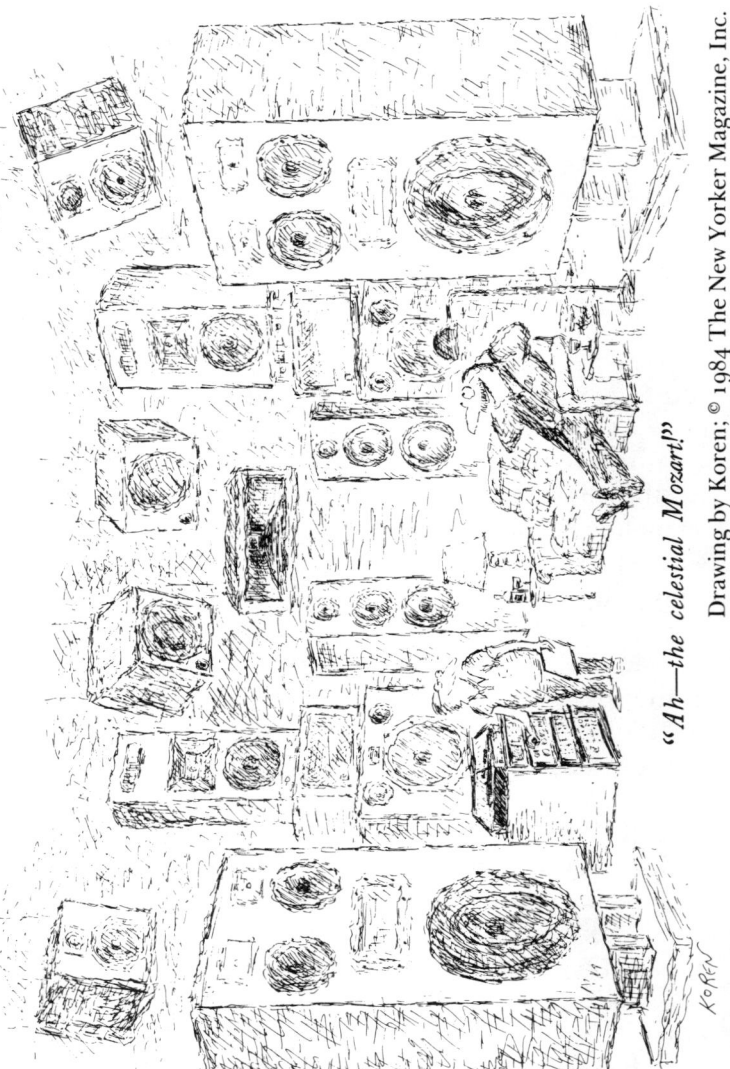

"*Ah—the celestial Mozart!*"

Drawing by Koren; © 1984 The New Yorker Magazine, Inc.

vigour of soul which no adverse experience, no poverty, worry, or illness, could take from him.

And just as the melodies of Tamino's flute prove their protective magic even in flames of fire and floods of water and their blessing descends on Pamina and Papageno, too, so to this day—and today perhaps more than ever—Mozart's music proves its beneficent, helpful, enchanting power with everyone to whom it speaks.

HERMANN HESSE

(1877–1962) was born in Wurttemberg, Germany, and began publishing distinguished novels as early as 1904 (*Peter Camenzind*) and 1906 (*Unterm Rad*). He moved to Switzerland before World War I, studied Neitzsche, and after the war visited India, an experience that resulted in the novel *Siddartha* (1923). His masterpiece, translated into many languages, is *Steppenwolf* (1927). He won the Nobel Prize for Literature in 1946.

From Steppenwolf:

. . . And I heard from the empty spaces within the theatre the sound of music, a beautiful and awful music, that music from *Don Giovanni* that heralds the approach of the guest of stone. With an awful and an iron clang it rang through the ghostly house, coming from the other world, from the immortals.

"Mozart," I thought, and with the word conjured up the most beloved and the most exalted picture that my inner life contained.

At that, there rang out behind me a peal of laughter, a clear and ice-cold laughter out of a world unknown to men, a world beyond all suffering, and born of divine humor. I turned about, frozen through with the blessing of this laughter, and there came Mozart. He passed by me laughing as he went and, strolling quietly on, he opened the door of one of the boxes and went in. Eagerly I followed the god of my youth, the object, all my life long, of love and veneration. The music rang on. Mozart was leaning over the front of the box. Of the theatre nothing was to be seen. Darkness filled the boundless space.

"You see," said Mozart, "it goes all right without the saxophone—though to be sure, I shouldn't wish to tread on the toes of that famous instrument."

"Where are we?" I asked.

"We are in the last act of *Don Giovanni*. Leporello is on his knees. A superb scene, and the music is fine too. There is a lot in it, certainly, that's very human, but you can hear the other world in it—the laughter, eh?"

"It is the last great music ever written," said I with the pomposity of a schoolmaster. "Certainly, there was Schubert to come. Hugo Wolf also, and I must not forget the poor, lonely Chopin either. You frown, Maestro? Oh, yes, Beethoven—he is wonderful too. But all that—beautiful as it may be—has something rhapsodical about it, something of disintegration. A work of such plenitude and power as *Don Giovanni* has never since arisen among men."

He raised his hands as though he were conducting, and a moon, or some pale constellation, rose somewhere. I looked over the edge of the box into immeasurable depths of space. Mist and clouds floated there. Mountains and seashores glimmered, and beneath us extended world-wide a desert plain. On this plain we saw an old gentleman of a worthy aspect, with a long beard, who drearily led a large following of some ten thousand men in black. He had a melancholy and hopeless air; and Mozart said:

"Look, there's Brahms. He is striving for redemption, but it will take him all his time."

I realized that the thousands of men in black were the players of all those notes and parts in his scores which according to divine judgment were superfluous.

"Too thickly orchestrated, too much material wasted," Mozart said with a nod.

And thereupon we saw Richard Wagner marching at the head of a host just as vast, and felt the pressure of those thousands as they clung and closed upon him. Him, too, we watched as he dragged himself along with slow and sad step.

"In my young days," I remarked sadly, "these two musicians passed as the most extreme contrasts conceivable."

Mozart laughed.

"Yes, that is always the way. Such contrasts, seen from a little distance, always tend to show their increasing similarity. Thick orchestration was in any case neither Wagner's nor Brahms' personal failing. It was a fault of their time."

(Later, Mozart) sat there and began busying himself with an apparatus and some instruments that stood beside him. He took it very seriously, tightening this and screwing that, and I looked with wonder at his adroit and nimble fingers and wished that I might see them playing a piano for once. I watched him thoughtfully, or in a reverie rather, lost in admiration of his beautiful and skillful hands, warmed too, by the sense of his presence and a little apprehensive as well. Of what he was actually doing and of what it was that he screwed and manipulated, I took no heed whatever.

I soon found, however, that he had fixed up a radio and put it in going order, and now he inserted the loudspeaker and said: "Munich is on the air. *Concerto Grosso in F Major* by Handel."

And in fact, to my indescribable astonishment and horror, the devilish tin trumpet spat out, without more ado, a mixture of bronchial slime and chewed rubber; that noise that owners of gramophones and radios have agreed to call music. And behind the slime and the croaking there was, sure enough, like an old master beneath a layer of dirt, the noble outline of that divine music. I could distinguish the majestic structure and the deep wide breadth and the full broad bowing of the strings.

"My God," I cried in horror, "what are you doing, Mozart? Do you really mean to inflict this mess on me and yourself, this triumph of our day, the last victorious weapon in the war of extermination against art? Must this be, Mozart?"

How the weird man laughed! And what a cold and eerie laugh! It was noiseless and yet everything was shattered by it. He marked my torment with deep satisfaction while he bent over the cursed screws and attended to the tin trumpet . . .

WALLACE STEVENS

(1879–1955) attended Harvard and New York University Law School, later becoming a successful insurance company executive, but his great interest was poetry which he produced as a second vocation, winning the poetry Pulitzer Prize in 1955, the year of his death.

MOZART, 1935

Poet, be seated at the piano.
Play the present, its hoo-hoo-hoo,
Its shoo-shoo-shoo, its ric-a-nic,
Its envious cachinnation.

If they throw stones upon the roof
While you practice arpeggios,
It is because they carry down the stairs
A body in rags.
Be seated at the piano.

That lucid souvenir of the past,
The divertimento;
That airy dream of the future,
The unclouded concerto . . .
The snow is falling.
Strike the piercing chord.

Be thou the voice,
Not you. Be thou, be thou
The voice of angry fear,
The voice of this besieging pain.

Be thou that wintry sound
As of the great wind howling,
By which sorrow is released,
Dismissed, absolved
In a starry placating.

We may return to Mozart.
He was young, and we, we are old.
The snow is falling
And the streets are full of cries.
Be seated, thou.

Bela Bartok

(1881–1945) of Hungarian birth, is thought by many to be one of this century's greatest composers. His piano concertos, ballets and chamber works are now played internationally, their unusual rhythms and tonal scales breaking away from the classical norms. His *Piano Concerto No. 2* (1931) and *No. 3* (1945) are among his often heard masterpieces.

Quoted in "The Life and Music of Bela Bartok" by Halsey Stevens:

Why do I make so little use of counterpoint? I was inclined to answer (you): because my beak grew that way (*weil mir der Schnabel so gewachen ist*). But since this is no answer, I shall attempt to clarify the situation: 1. In any case this is its character in performance; 2. In my youth my ideal of beauty was not so much the art of Bach or Mozart as that of Beethoven. Recently it has changed somewhat . . .

IGOR STRAVINSKY

(1882–1971) was born near St. Petersburg, Russia and, like Tchaikovsky before him, reluctantly studied for the law until in 1902 he met Rimsky-Korsakov whose music instruction soon paid off as Stravinsky began to write the remarkable series of works still acclaimed the world over, *The Firebird Suite* (1910), *Petrouchka* (1911) and the later masterpieces, *The Rite of Spring* (1913), string quartets, operas and even music for the motion pictures after Stravinsky moved to Los Angeles.

From "Retrospectives & Conclusions" by Igor Stravinsky and Robert Craft:

I have just completed the *Rex Tremendae* of my pocket *Requiem*. I call it that both because I use only fragments of the text, and interlard them with instrumental music (though there is precious little lard in it), and because most of it was composed in notebooks which I carry in my pockets. But I am superstitious and do not like to talk about any work in progress, let alone a monument ordered, like Mozart's, by a "mysterious stranger."

(Regarding *The Magic Flute*): Certainly the *magic* is limited to the music, while the moral meaning—

the entity I believe in—would hardly be worth stating, if it could be stated, apart from it. Still, the music is not "independent," and not "pure." In fact, it seems to me that the intentional meaning of the opera, the triumph of Life over Death, is reversed at times in the depths of the music; in the brave little parade of Music through the gates of Death, for example, the flute charms the Keeper into a stay of execution, but the piece is a funeral march, nonetheless. Death is just beneath the surface in much of the other music as well, especially Pamina's; and in the great C-minor fugato-chorale, which somehow succeeds in sounding Beethoven's *Eroica* note without Beethoven's display of superior will, the wings of the terrible angel are closer than they have ever been before in music.

Mozart's Masonic allegory-land is a more attractive country than the *dix-huitieme* Establishment countries of his other operas, at least to me, and not only musically. It is morally more generous, for one thing, and for another the dramatic terrain ranges more widely, partly because of the new and diverse elevations of the religious, the mystical, and the supernatural. In fact, the greatest achievement of the opera is precisely the entity, the unity of feeling that embues all of the music from sacred choruses and magic spells to the proto-Broadway duet—except in musical quality—concerning the future propagations of Papageno and Papagena.

Unlike *Don Giovanni* the opera does not include any extended scene, but neither does it "lack" one. (It also does not include, or lack, any bore comparable to Masetto.) On the other hand, Mozart is more economical and faster-moving than ever, setting the stage for the final scene, for instance, with a single phrase. The simplest means are more effective too, as in the device of the "false" relationship, which occurs in all of his music, yet here (most vertiginously in Pamina's "*Mir klingt der Mutternahme susse*") as if for the first time.

The most obvious anticipations are of Weber, Wagner, the Mendelssohn of the *Midsummer Night's Dream*. (The most obvious omission is Schubert, who had already been scooped in "*L'ho perduta*" from *Figaro*.) Wagner is everywhere, and all the way from *Tannhauser* (the sixteenth-note violin figuration in the final *Andante*) to *Tristan* ("*Wann also wird die Decke Schwinden*" and "*jeden Tone meinen Dank zu schildern*"). The Pamino-Sarastro scene is Wagnerian, too (though Sarastro's own music more strikingly resembles the music of Jesus in the Bach Passions), except that Mozart stops at the point where Wagner, already heavy-breathing, would have begun to overblow.

ARTUR SCHNABEL

(1882–1951) was born in Lipnik, Austria, was a naturalized American (1944) who became one of the world's leading concert pianists, recording all the piano works of Beethoven and most of Mozart, concertizing with many of the world's greatest conductors and orchestras.

From "Artur Schnabel" by Cesar Saerchinger:

It is interesting and revealing that Schnabel, while in the midst of his Beethoven studies, and while preparing himself for the monumental task of playing the entire thirty-two sonatas in Berlin, deliberately turned aside to take a fresh look at Mozart, a composer whose works for the piano he had hardly touched since the days of his childhood when he, like most beginners, was given Mozart to 'cut his teeth on.' He recalled, with something like horror, how at the age of nine he had been made to play the master's D minor concerto as a proficiency test for the benefit of his Viennese sponsors. 'Children are given Mozart,' he used to say, 'because of the quantity of the notes; grown-ups avoid him because of the *quality* of the notes, which to be sure, is elusive.'

... in his later years Schnabel spent an inconceivable amount of time and effort in convincing sceptics of the supreme mastery and profundity of Mozart, and in impressing students with the difficulty of playing his works.

It was after he had finished work on his Beethoven edition that he seriously investigated the lesser-known Mozart concertos. And, as with Schubert and Beethoven, the discovery made him a pioneer. From that time onward he was wont to add at least one new Mozart concerto to his repertoire every year until he had played some twelve of them in public, and many of them a number of times. Later in life he often made the inclusion of Mozart concertos a condition of his acceptance of orchestral engagements, and in after years he played two or even three Mozart concertos at a single concert. Exacting and meticulous as he was at rehearsals—until he was assured that the orchestra's performance was commensurate with his own and, if possible, that the orchestral players really enjoyed it! Mozart, he insisted, was inconceivable without love—on the part of all participants. . . .

Again and again in later life he inveighed against people who thought of Mozart as something less than profound, while admitting his charm, his supposed simplicity and graceful 'rococo' character. 'Mozart is not for candlelight,' he once said when someone suggested eighteenth-century period trimmings for a concert. 'He is the sun.' 'Mozart's music is universal he wrote in his early sixties. 'It is transcendental and representative, above time and locality. It is the symbol of man's position in the universe and his reaction to the universe. It is the best that man can accomplish.'

ZOLTAN KODALY

(1882–1967), a native of Kicskemet, Hungary, is associated with Bela Bartok as an exponent of Hungarian folk music. He composed a large body of work in all forms, from opera, chamber and choral to orchestral and vocal music. More conservative than Bartok, his style found early acceptance, and his *Hary Janos Suite* (1926) and *Dances of Galanta* (1933) are more 'traditional' music than that of his friend Bartok.

From "The Selected Writings of Zoltan Kodaly":

A small child will often hum senseless words (senseless, that is, for us), and enjoy the purely musical kaleidoscope, as if it were a handful of colored pebbles. That is why he loves meaningless refrains . . . But if Mozart—a genius—enjoyed at the age of three or four a song with a meaningless text he had invented himself, why should we deprive the three/four year olds who will not become Mozarts of this pleasure?

A cultured musician can study Raphael's Madonnas as profitably as a cultured painter can study Mozart's symphonies, wrote Robert Schumann.

Charles T. Griffes

(1884–1920) was born in Elmyra, New York, studied piano from boyhood and continued this work in Germany under Engelbert Humperdinck (composer of the opera *Hansel and Gretel*). His great promise was not actually fulfilled, and at age 36 after a brief illness he died leaving several highly regarded works including *The Pleasure Dome of Kubla Khan* (1919) and *The White Peacock* (1917).

From "Charles T. Griffes" by Edward M. Maisel:

(In a letter to Miss Broughton, November 18, ———) That night of the company, when we played the Mozart quartet, Dr. Landau said I was a Mozart player—which was a fine compliment, I think.

(In a letter to the same, February 4,———) . . . I stayed home and played and worked some on a piece I am arranging for piano. It is a piece of Mozart's which Herr Galton let me take, and which is originally for a large sort of music box, called a musical clock. It has been arranged for orchestra and for two pianos, but Galston thought not yet for piano solo, so he said it might be good practice for me.

There is a certain resemblance (in Griffes' end) to Mozart's death, of which a French doctor has written: "Two factors hastened Mozart's death. The first was a chronic cause, dating from his earliest years and increasing every day. This was simply excessive work, continual fatigue, and profound misery. One should be able to say of a man as of a machine: 'This machine is used up, it has been worked too much.' The word *used* applies perfectly to Mozart. Mozart arrived at the age of thirty-five worn out, having expended all his vital power. It was at that moment that the disease which carried him off laid hold of him."

ALBAN BERG

(1892–1974), born in Vienna, studied under Schoenberg by whom he was greatly influenced, using that composer's twelve-tone scale. He wrote among many lesser works for orchestra and strings, the operas *Wozzek* (1925) and *Lulu* (1936), both often performed today.

Quoted in "The Life and work of Alban Berg" by Willi Reich, translated by Cornelius Cardew:

... our taste is all too easily corrupted by all the music that's simply flung together these days—and then highly praised by newspapers and public. Something really good is acknowledged only later on—if it happens early it's mostly just a matter of fashion! The masses have now arrived at R. Wagner—he deserves it!! They only respect the earlier masters—Bach, Beethoven, Mozart—because it would be a scandal if they didn't. But I wouldn't like to look into the souls of these people who applaud a Bach concerto, a late Beethoven quartet or even a Mozart aria or minuet with such enthusiasm, for fear of seeing the deadly boredom there.

One would either have to be very deaf or very malicious to describe a music (Schoenberg's) that manifests such richness of rhythms (and in such a concentrated form both successively and simultaneously) as 'arhythmic.' If this word is intended to refer to all relations of temp and note-values that are not directly derivable from mechanical movement (e.g., mill-wheel or railway train) or from bodily movement (e.g., marching, dancing, etc.) then by all means call Schoenberg's music 'arhythmic.' But then the word must also be applied to the music of Mozart and all the classical masters except when they purposely aimed at uniform and therefore easily comprehensible rhythms, as in their dances and the movements derived from old dance forms (Scherzo, Rondo, etc.).

SERGE PROKOFIEV

(1891–1953) at 6 years of age composed a waltz, a march and a rondo, confirming his status as another child prodigy. Born in Ekaterinoslav district of Russia, by the age of 12 he had written two operas, leading his parents to believe him worthy to be placed under the tutelage of Rimsky-Korsakov and Gliere. Leaving Russia at the time of the Bolshevik revolution, he lived much of his life in Paris where such works as the *Lieutenant Kije Suite* (1934) and *Peter and the Wolf* (1936) were composed. His symphonies and operas are often performed, and he is regarded as one of Russia's great masters.

From "Sergei Prokofiev, a Soviet Tragedy" by Victor Seroff:

The cultivated young officer (Nikolai Miaskovsky) did not cry "anathema" when Sergei confessed that he did not like Mozart because of his "oversimple harmonization" or Chopin because he was "much too sweet." . . . For a while Madame Essipova overlooked Sergei's disrespectful attitude toward certain composers: "They say one cannot give a piano recital without playing Chopin, and I am going to prove that one can." He treated Mozart with even more disdain: "What primitive, monotonous harmony." . . . Essipova forced him to play Mozart, Schubert, and Chopin, insisting on finely polished execution of every piece.

"Thus I fell into the category of students devoid of talent," Sergei said later. "And although during my Conservatory days I managed to conduct the school orchestra in public performances of Schubert's Unfinished Symphony, Beethoven's Seventh Symphony, and even Mozart's *The Marriage of Figaro*, I didn't feel 'at home' at the conductor's desk." Only much later, after his graduation from the Conservatory, did Sergei acquire sufficient experience in leading an orchestra. But what was more important, through his work in the conducting class under Tcherepnin, he mastered the art of orchestration.

"Tcherepnin's role in my general education was of paramount value to me: he spoke of innovation in compositions in such a way that I felt like a backward musician; his analytical remarks on opera became very useful in my writing of operas. With a score in his hands, sitting next to me at innumerable rehearsals of the school orchestra, he would point out: 'Listen to how beautiful the bassoon sounds here' or, 'Did you notice the English horn?' I began to acquaire a taste for the scores of Haydn and Mozart, hence later on came my Classical Symphony."

"As one listens to The Gambler (an opera), one receives a pleasure similar to that derived from Mozart, except that it is written in a contemporary medium."

Hearing an explanation of the story of Sheridan's *The Duenna*, Prokofiev exclaimed, "But this is champagne! One can make an opera out of this in the style of Mozart, Rossini!" And he immediately set to work on it.

Prokofiev wrote: "Let us consider the creative

activities of Beethoven and Shakespeare, Mozart and Tolstoy, Tchaikovsky and Dickens—those titans of the human spirit and thought. Does their greatness not consist precisely in the fact that these men of their own free will gave their mighty talent to the service of mankind?

Rebecca West

(Cicily Isabel Fairfield) (1892–1983) was born in London of Scotch parentage and became a journalist interested in political reform and feminism. She was emotionally involved for many years with H. G. Wells by whom she had a son, Anthony West. She wrote many novels and *belles lettres*, but her *magnum opus* is *Black Lamb and Grey Falcon* (1941), a compendium of travel observations and thoughts on many things sublunary, described by the critic Samuel Hynes as "a supreme effort, by a mind at the height of its powers."

From "Black Lamb and Grey Falcon":

We none of us knew what to say or do, but just at that moment someone turned on the radio and the restaurant was flooded with a symphony by Mozart, and we all forgot Gerda. Constantine began to hum the theme, and his plump little hands followed the flight of Mozart's spirit as at Yaitse they had followed the motion of the bird at the waterfall. We all drew on the comfort which is given out by the major works of Mozart, which is as real and material as the warmth given by a glass of brandy, and I wondered, seeing its efficacy, what its nature might be. It is in part, no doubt, the work of the technical trick by which Mozart eliminates the idea of haste from life. His airs could not lag as they make their journey through the listener's attention; they are not the right shape for loitering. But it is true that they never rush, they are never headlong or helter-skelter, they splash no mud, they raise no dust. It is, indeed, inadequate to call the means of creating such an effect a mere technical device. For it changes the content of the work in which it is used, it presents a vision of a world where man is no longer the harrassed victim of time but accepts its discipline and establishes a harmony with it. This is not a little thing, for our struggle with time is one of the most distressing of our fundamental conflicts, it holds us back from the achievement and comprehension that should be the justification for our life. How heavily this struggle weighs on us may be judged from certain of our preferences. Whatever our belief in the supernatural may be, we all feel that Christ was something that St. Paul was not; and it is impossible to imagine Christ hurrying, while it is impossible to imagine St. Paul doing anything else.

Darius Milhaud

(1892–1974), born in Aix-en-Provence, France, entered the Paris Conservatory in 1909 and soon became a member of Les Six, young composers who experimented with unusual tonal forms. He lived and worked in California for several years, returning to teach at the Paris Conservatory after 1947. His best known works are the early ballets, *La Creation du Monde* (1923) and *Le Boeuf sur le Toit* (1919).

From "An Autobiography, Notes Without Music" by Darius Milhaud:

(At the 1937 Paris International Exposition) the National Broadcasting System had a studio with walls of glass so that the public could see all that was going on. The broadcasts were relayed over the whole exposition by means of a system of loudspeakers, and music seemed to have found its natural home in space. One autumn evening I listened to the pure crystalline notes of one of Mozart's concertos dropping at our feet like leaves from the trees.

VIRGIL THOMSON

(1896–) was born in Kansas City, Missouri, is well known for his voluminous writings about music (critic on the *New York Herald Tribune* from 1940 to 1954), but he also composed ballets, symphonies and chamber music as well as operas. Gertrude Stein wrote the lyrics for his *Four Saints in Three Acts* (1927) and *The Mother of Us All* (1947) that hold the stage today.

From "Virgil Thomson" by Virgil Thomson:

From then on I played the piano constantly, recovering my lost finger skills and mastering a whole batch of Mozart sonatas. Mozart was a major problem in those days; and restudying his works, forging a new style for playing them which would be convincing to a music world longing to hear them rendered with a grandeur appropriate to their proportions, had replaced the Bach problem of thirty years before. Well into June I kept up my investigations, discovering, I think, something like a method for solving the expressive content of any Mozart piece. At least I made sure that there *is* an expressive content, and never since have I been tolerant toward an "abstract" or "absolute" approach to this composer.

ROGER SESSIONS

(1896–1985) was born in Brooklyn, New York, and taught at several colleges in the United States (Smith, California, Princeton) while composing in almost all genres, using the atonal idiom so that his work is often referred to as 'American modern,' exemplified in his *Symphony No. 3* (1957), *Violin Concerto* (1935) and *Rhapsody for Orchestra* (1970).

From "Composers on Music" edited by Sam Morgenstern:

The past is never, as our jargon implies, a fixed quantity; it is in movement. If we regard it clearly, we see it moving toward us, and if we set out to meet it, we find that it sees itself quite differently from the way we see it. Mozart, for his contemporaries, was not the serene classic, the apostle of measure and perfection, that so many of his admirers of the nineteenth century, and even some of those of today, have liked to conjure up. On the contrary, he was for them a painter of intense and even sombre canvases, of large scope and vast design, whom Lorenzo da Ponte is said on one occasion to have coupled in comparison with Dante of the *Inferno*.

VINCENT SHEEAN

(1899–1975), born in Pana, Illinois, was a well known journalist and newspaper correspondent. His *Personal History* was a best seller of 1935. He has written, "I am excessively fond of music and used often to go without food to buy tickets to concerts and operas."

From "First Love and Last" by Vincent Sheean:

I heard *Figaro* for the first time in my life . . . at the Opera House in Dusseldorf and was played by the company from Cologne. The sheer loveliness of the music needed no gloss and I knew at once that this must be a source of never ending delight. Although my own ignorance of the work and of Mozart's operas in general was complete and I thus had no standard, I could hear and see the exquisite care with which every note had been prepared, the wonderfully apposite but restrained stage direction, the fresh, pretty settings and dresses. Nothing so good as this *Figaro* would have been possible in the Paris of that day or, I suspect, any other, because these agreeable voices (none great or famous) were beautifully styled and blended. No sight or sound was ugly and the evening was, I have often thought since, one of the most satisfactory I have ever spent in an opera theatre. One's first *Figaro* comes only once, and I was lucky that it came in such a guise.

Coming back from Jerusalem in the autumn of 1929 I stopped for a week or two in Vienna and heard, among other things, *Cosi fan Tutte* and *Die Entfuhrung aus dem Serail*, both for the first time. Clemens Kraus had just become general director of the Vienna Opera that year, and *Cosi fan Tutte* was one of his new productions (I think his first). I loved it at first sight or sound. *Die Entfuhrung* was almost equally a delight, and at some moments—with Schumann singing Blondchen—even more. I thought then that Mozart could never be played anywhere so well as in Vienna or Salzburg. It is a tenable position at any time, but his music yields itself so flexibly to treatment by any qualified group of singers and musicians that I am not so sure now. I have heard excellent Mozart in Italy, England, America and even in France I have heard good amateur performances. Bernard Shaw once made a complicated journey by bus, underground and other means to the Isle of Dogs, in the Thames River at the thither extremity of the East End, to hear *Die Zauberflote* performed by a cast of boys and girls from a social settlement under the direction of their clergyman; he told me it was excellent.

I have said . . . that *Tristan und Isolde* is for me one of the supreme aesthetic experiences of a lifetime. It goes into the same category (for me—I speak only for myself) as Michelangelo's work in the Sistine

VIVA MOZART

Chapel, Bach's in the *St. John Passion* and the *B Minor Mass*, Mozart's in *Don Giovanni*, and Shakespeare's in *Macbeth*. These are the highest values in that mystery called art, the work of man which most approaches the work of God.

. . . has anybody now alive failed to notice how much of the work of Mozart is being performed all over the world in the year 1956? Why? Because it is the two hundredth anniversary of his birth—that is the reason given. It may be a reason but I think it is only an excuse. At the present moment every artist in the world of music, with no exception I can readily call to mind, has a vast Mozart repertoire. Every pianist, violinist, chamber-music player, orchestral conductor, singer and virtuoso of every description has Mozart treasure to give forth. Without the slightest difficulty you can get up a good program of Mozart's music anywhere on earth where there are musicians. It could not have happened even so much as twenty-five years ago. When I was growing up, and indeed until I was in my thirties, there were hardly any opportunities to hear Mozart's work in the opera houses; the symphonies and some chamber music were currently performed, although not as they are today.

Bernard Shaw says there exists a short story by Richard Wagner, somewhere in his immense collected works (I have never been able to find it), in which a dying musician, visited by a spiritual adviser on his deathbed, makes a confession of faith. "I believe in God, Mozart and Beethoven," he says.

GEORGE ANTHEIL

(1900–1959), a native of Trenton, New Jersey, at 22 won a Guggenheim Fellowship and concertized throughout Europe as pianist. His music expressed the cacophony of modern life, especially his early *Ballet Mecanique* (1924). Writing for motion pictures his scores became less daring, and he turned to the symphony and opera.

From "Composers on Music" edited by Sam Morgenstern:

The "fun" in a Mozart symphony is not entirely unlike that of a baseball game. In baseball all plays are severely within the rules; what would you think of a baseball team that had twenty-seven players instead of nine? Baseball operates strictly within the rules, and to make certain that the rules are kept, umpires stand right on the field.

The composers of the hundred or more years preceding the overlap of the Chopin-Schumann-Wagner romantic period derived their main excitement, their top spiritual exaltation, from the masterly way in which they could knock out home runs or move and skip about inside of these binding, limiting classic rules.

Mozart's mastery was so superb, so utterly topnotch, that Mozart fans experienced exactly the same sensation which a modern baseball audience might

Aaron Copland

(1900–   ) was born in Brooklyn, New York. In his teens he studied under Goldmark ("Rustic Wedding") and later in Paris with Nadia Boulanger. In addition to orchestral, piano and choral works, he composed the now standard American ballets, *Billy the Kid* (1939), *Rodeo* (1942) and *Appalachian Spring* (1944).

From "Composers on Music" edited by Sam Morgenstern:

My love of the music of Chopin and Mozart is as strong as that of the next fellow, but it does me little good when I sit down to write my own, because their world is not mine and their language not mine. The underlying principles of their music are just as cogent today as they were in their own period, but the essential point is that with these same principles, one may and one does produce a quite different result.

Vladimir Horowitz

(1904–   ), one of the world's foremost pianists, was born in the Ukraine, became a United States citizen in 1944, and after years of concertizing to great acclaim on every continent, retired in 1953, only to emerge from time to time by public demand. In his 80's he made headline news by returning to Russia in a memorable solo appearance that was televised internationally.

From "Great Pianists Speak for Themselves" by Elyse Mach:

(Horowitz said:) I believe that Clementi influenced Beethoven more than any other composer. There's no doubt about it; he was a great musician, although he does have some sonatas which are not very interesting. Clementi also composed quite a number of symphonies, twenty-five or thirty, I think, but he burned them after learning of a letter Mozart wrote criticizing his writing efforts in this direction. It seems that he learned of this letter's existence and possible publication so, as a devotee of Mozart, he burned them. Certainly Mozart had more genius than Clementi. Why, Mozart even built a new piano and influenced what could actually be played on it. His concerti are works of genius, and his sonatas are lovely too, but some are not at all interesting. They are played anyway because they have a good signature.

W. H. Auden

(1907–1973) a naturalized American citizen, born in England where he became the most famous of the poets in the Louis MacNeice, C. Day Lewis, Stephen Spender group, came to the United States at the outset of World War II, and moved steadily from liberalism to conservative views.

From "W. H. Auden, a Biography" by Humphrey Carpenter:

Auden had been brought up, despite his enthusiasm for music, to be almost totally ignorant of opera—'to think' as he put it, 'that opera was impossible.' This attitude was typical of his parents' generation in England, which believed, as he said, that 'the great Mozart operas might just do because Mozart was Mozart,' but regarded Wagner and Verdi as vulgar and considered Rossini, Bellini and Donizetti to be 'simply beyond the pale.' . . . Less than a year (later) Auden wrote to a friend in England, 'My chief luxury is the opera.'

JACQUES BARZUN

(1907–) was born in France, came to the United States and graduated from Columbia College in 1927, joining its history department in the same year. Later for 12 years he was Provost of Columbia University and named University Professor in 1967, retiring from the university in 1975. A past president of the National Institute of Arts and Letters, he is author of such standard works as *Darwin, Marx, Wagner; Berlioz and the Romantic Century; A Stroll with William James*; and many others.

From the Introduction to "Pleasures of Music" by Jacques Barzun:

. . . there is more truth (and more fun) embodied in the few pages of a letter by Mozart, in a jotting by Delacroix, or a portrait by Romain Rolland, than in the combined utterances of ten generations of "sober judges" and "competent musicians."

Erich Leinsdorf

(1912–) was born in Vienna and is one of the great conductors known internationally, leading such orchestras as the Metropolitan Opera, Boston Symphony, Cleveland, New York Philharmonic, Vienna, Berlin, and Los Angeles, and he has recorded, among others, all the symphonies of Mozart, Beethoven and Brahms.

From an Interview reported in the San Jose Mercury, January 24, 1984:

Keeping up the old style is a major Leinsdorf tenet. "I am worried about keeping up Mozart—and Wagner already." He makes it a point now to include some Mozart (such as tonight's Symphony No. 38) on every orchestral program. "Mozart becomes greater, the more you know him. No other composer has the same range, from the most sublime to the most bawdy." He declines to speculate on the premise that Mozart lived a full life, and did not die at the age of 35. But he quotes one Australian philosopher who opined that great creative talents died young because they burned themselves out—that in effect their life was complete in their own eyes.

From "Cadenza—A Musical Career" by Erich Leinsdorf:

I had the reputation, buttressed by the Tanglewood weeks of Mozart and more Mozart, of having a special affinity for Wolfgang Amadeus. My albums with the forty-one symphonies had been well received (and have lasted on the market for two decades). My own advisers pressed me to record Mozart and Haydn, not only great music but more popular with many young record collectors than the Brahms and Tchaikovsky repertoire. RCA was more than willing if they did not have to pay for 106 players when 50 perform.

When Henryk Szeryng played the Brahms Concerto with me in London it was quite clear that people wanted to applaud after the first movement. As the clapping started, the solist in all his dignity, with his instrument always under his chin, raised his right arm and held the bow in a gesture of such peremptory shock that no high priest in whose inner sanctum a sacrilege had been committed could improve on it. What utter nonsense. The notion, once entertained by questionable historians, was that an entity must not be interrupted by the mundane frivolity of hand clapping. The great composers were elated by applause, wherever it burst out. Mozart even wrote with glee of an occasion when the Parisians, surprised and delighted by a turn in composition, applauded in the middle of a movement.

BENJAMIN BRITTEN

(1913–1976) was born in Lowestoft, England, and early showed great musical ability. His operas, *Albert Herring* (1947), *Peter Grimes* (1945), and *Billy Budd* (1951) are now standard works in opera repertory worldwide.

From "Britten" by Imogen Holst:

In one of his program notes about Mozart, he (Britten) has said: 'All his life, Mozart had the wit to be influenced by great composers, but then he assimilated these influences and made them part of his own character.

When you hear of an artist saying or doing something strange or unpopular, think of that extra sensitivity—that skin less; consider a moment whether he may not after all be seeing a little more clearly than ourselves, whether he is really as irresponsible as he seems, before you condemn him. Remember for a moment Mozart in his pauper's grave; Dostoievsky sent to Siberia; Blake ridiculed as a madman . . . It is a proud privilege to be a creative artist, but it can also be painful.

From "Benjamin Britten, His Life and Operas" by Eric Walter White:

In his broadcast talk *The Composer and the Listener* (1946) he (Britten) said: 'Obviously it is no use having a technique unless you have the ideas to use this technique . . . There has never been a composer worth his salt who has not had supreme technique. I'll go further than that and say that in the work of your supreme artist you can't separate inspiration from technique. I'd like anyone to tell me where Mozart's inspiration ends and technique begins.'

Britten was prepared to oblige with every type of

music, light or serious . . . He was often able to complete the greater part of the composition of a new work in his mind so that (as was the case with Mozart) the act of committing it to paper became an almost mechanical process which could be carried out at high speed.

(Britten said) 'I actually started work on the opera (*A Midsummer Night's Dream*) in October, and finished it on, I think, Good Friday—seven months for everything, including the score. This is not up to the speed of Mozart or Verdi, but these days, when the line of musical language is broken, it is much rarer.'

RANDALL JARRELL

(1914–1965) a native of Tennessee, graduated from Vanderbilt University and became a member of the literary group associated with the *Kenyon Review* and Southern poets and critics.

THE AUGSBURG ADORATION

Mozart, Goethe, and the Duke of Wellington
Spent the night at the Drei Mohren; so did we.
Did the Duke of Wellington find by his bed
Two bananas and two sugar-cubes, as we did?
Did the sparrows cheep, cheep, cheep to get
   the sugar?

And did Mozart sleep, next night, beside the highest
Spire in all the world—unfinished then? Ulm's emblem
Is a sparrow holding in its beak a straw.
You can buy it, in chocolate, at the bakeries.

Did Goethe see, among the cobblestones, the Roman
Manhole-covers marked SPQR? For the breath
Of those letters, the Senate and the People
Lived for us, indomitable as the sparrows
The bread-eating cats stalked in the ruins
   of Rome.

Travellers, we come to Rome, Ulm, Augsburg,
To adore something; the child nursing at the stone
Breast beside a stone ox, stone ass, a flesh-and-blood
Sparrow who nests in the manger. The Three Kings
Bring him stones and stones and stones, the sparrow
Brings a straw. The years have worn away the stone,
But the bird cramming food into the beseeching
Mouth in its nest of rubbish, is as perfect
As when the child first said of Mozart, Goethe,
And the Iron Duke: *One of them shall not fall*
On the ground without your Father. They have fallen

And the sparrow has not fallen. The straw-bearing
Sparrow at Ulm, at Augsburg, is indistinguishable
In its perfection from the sparrow who brought straw
To its nest, food to its young, in Rome, in Nazareth—
The green Forum's sparrows are the sparrows of home.

Yehudi Menuhin

(1916–) grew up in the San Francisco Bay Area, and at age 4 took violin lessons. At age 8 he performed on the concert stage, in 1927 playing Beethoven's Violin Concerto in New York under Fritz Busch, gaining national acclaim and has held renown as one of the world's foremost violinists.

From "Yehudi Menuhin" by Robert Magidoff. Told by Magidoff in connection with Menuhin's learning the A Major Violin Concerto when he was 8 years old:

. . . in his childhood and adolescence, Yehudi played Mozart with an unequalled purity and perfection which proved more elusive in later years, although at the same time his performance of other composers grew in depth and beauty.

"Even as a young boy," Menuhin said by way of an explanation, "I knew a great deal about Mozart, both from his music and from books, and I worshipped him. The initial carelessness with which I treated the A-major was due largely to my vanity—I was eager to get on to Beethoven, but the moment I surmounted that superficial attitude and immersed myself in the music, I discovered a greater affinity with Mozart than with any other composer. Psychologically, at the time he was the most immediately available composer to me, for his style had crystallized when he was still a child, and remained true to its undefiled simplicity, although it later grew in richness and subtlety. Mozart's appeal to me was as child to child and as innocence to innocence. Guided by the instinctive inspiration and devotion of youth, one can play Beethoven with great beauty and even with a degree of penetration, but, without having first lived, no musician can render him perfectly. A young person, however, can play Mozart with perfection, as if touched by a magic wand. In order to penetrate his music and communicate it to the listener, I did not have to transpose myself—I could play him and remain myself, with no need to feel big, powerful, and grown-up; I did not even have to imagine myself in love.

Had I been reared on movies, comic strips, and other such crude sophistications of American life, I should probably have been robbed of the spontaneity and innocence without which Mozart cannot truthfully be conveyed. In fact, our entire present-day civilization lacks these qualities, which perhaps, accounts for the decline of the Mozart vogue in the United States(!). The moderns may be, and are capable of appreciating the heroic tragedy and noble suffering of a Beethoven, but the tender sorrow of Mozart is alien to them. For them, it is difficult to tell the difference between the simple and the affectedly simple, between the elegant and the sham elegant, even as it is to distinguish between a sweet girl and a coy one.

The emancipated modern man is so accustomed to seeing powerful emotions break the bonds of form in the arts that he finds it embarrassing to identify himself with such emotions when they are contained within a traditional framework. Mozart was able, because of the rigid conventions of his age, to pour his very genuine feelings into vessels the sheer elegance of which restrained their contents. He thus resolved his emotions on a level that transformed them into moods uncontaminated by mortal anguish. The child who never ceased to live within Mozart led him to sublimate his adult emotions into those he could have experienced had he never grown out of childhood.

Thus, from without, in terms of form, he inherited the elegance and grace of the court; from within, he had the qualities and attitudes of childhood—an age capable of suffering, but a suffering which does not sear or distort, enabling Mozart to express the 'angelic anguish' that is so peculiarly his own.

From "Unfinished Journey" by Yehudi Menuhin:

. . . I recall noting as a child that even a less than first-rate French orchestra could invariably do justice to Mozart, whereas all but the best German orchestras punished his delicacy with a heavy hand, a comparison which taught me that Mozart could be appreciated only in a chivalrous tradition.

Leonard Bernstein

(1918–   ) was born in Lawrence, Massachusetts and studied with Walter Piston, Randall Thompson and Serge Koussevitsky, becoming conductor at the Tanglewood concerts. At age 25 he was a conductor of the New York Philharmonic, appointed permanent conductor of that orchestra in 1958. As a composer his greatest successes have been in musical comedy, and *On theTown* (1944), *Candide* (1956) and *West Side Story* (1957) are an honorable part of Broadway history.

From "The Infinite Variety of Music" by Leonard Bernstein:

When we see all this (this breath-taking jewel of an opera house, known as La Fenice), what is it we hear? What is the first sound in our inner ears? Mozart, of course, who represents to most of us elegance, wit, daintiness, intimacy, and the rest. If this were all, however, then Mozart would have remained always an artist of his time, a rococo genius who captured his epoch in notes. But, then, so did some other composers called Stamitz and Dittersdorf capture their epoch in notes, and so did a lot of other names you may never have heard of, including several of old Johann Sebastian Bach's sons. . . . But today they are mostly just admired names, while Mozart is, and always will be, the divine Mozart: not a name, but a heavenly spirit who arrived in this world, remained some thirty-odd years, and then left it new, enriched, and blessed by his visit.

What makes this difference? Only this: that Mozart's genius was a universal one, like that of all great artists. He captured not only the feel and smell and spirit of his age but also the spirit of man, man of all epochs, man in all the subtleties of his desire, struggle, and ambivalence.

I heard the great Boris Pasternak say, "In spite of everything I am full of joy; my art exists as a record of the tragedy of human existence; it is nourished by tragedy; and my art is all my joy." So it is with our greatest creative spirits; so it is with Mozart. Which may come as something of a surprise to some of you who have the habit of equating Mozart with aristocratic delicacy and nothing more. How many people have I heard dismiss him as "tinkly," as a musical snuff-box composer! . . . Tinkly is it? Why, it could easily be Beethoven in one of his typically tragic rages. It has the power, the attack of a giant . . .

Mozart's music is constantly escaping from its frame, because it cannot be contained within it. No matter how clearly every bar of it is labeled 1779 or 1784, the music is essentially timeless. It is classical music by a great romantic. It is eternally modern music by a great classicist.

Now if you go through the complete works of Mozart, some rainy afternoon, you will find to your horror the same cadence—patterns used with incredible repetitiveness in work after work, movement after movement, even phrase after phrase. These cadences are almost no longer music; they seem to have become only points of punctuation.... No modern composer would ever permit himself such stock-in-trade repetition. (Except bad ones, mainly of the avant-garde.) What does it mean? That Mozart was played out? That he lacked inventiveness? Certainly not. Invention was Mozart's middle name. It means only that he was a composer of his time, that his vocabulary was necessarily delimited by the conventions of his time. The wonder is not that he used conventional formulas, but that, using them, he was able to create such amazing variety....

I don't know if you are familiar with the great C Major Piano Concerto, whose second movement begins with ... triplets. But when an unbelievable melodic line begins to soar above it, the mechanical little accompaniment becomes in itself a thing of rare beauty, especially orchestrated as it is with delicious pizzicato basses and subtle woodwind reinforcement. I find it one of the special treasures of all musical history ... What an extraordinary experience that melody is—timeless, ageless; and yet it rests on a rigid, formal eighteenth-century pedestal.

Such are some of the ways in which Mozart constantly moves above and beyond his period, bursting out of his formulistic frame, and even using those very formulas in his own way to produce music of surprising originality and power. It is a power that enabled him to produce works of towering strength, far indeed from the musical snuff-box in which people so often lock him up.

Mozart is *all* music; there is nothing you can ask from music that he cannot supply . . . If I absolutely *had* to name my all-time favorite piece of music, I think I would vote for the Andante (to the Piano Concerto in G Major). It is Mozart at the peak of his lyrical powers, combining serenity, melancholy, and tragic intensity in one great lyric improvisation. You will hear the tranquillity of a Schubert *Lied*, the filigree of a Chopin, the brooding of a Mahler . . . And . . . the Finale. Brilliant—that is the word for this marvelous rococo set of variations. The whole movement is bathed in a glitter that could have come only from the eighteenth century, from that age of light, lightness, and enlightenment. It is a perfect product of the age of reason—witty, objective, graceful, delicious. And yet, over it all hovers the greater spirit that is Mozart's—the spirit of compassion, of universal love, even of suffering—a spirit that knows no age, that belongs to all ages.

RUDOLF FIRKUSNY

(1924–) was born in Napajedla, Czechoslovakia, and at age 5 began instruction at the keyboard under Janacek. At age 10 he made his concert debut in Prague; in 1938 he made his first tour in the United States, is today an American citizen, lives in New York and teaches at the Juilliard School while concertizing extensively with major European and American orchestras.

"You are guilty of fraudulent advertising! You really *don't* like Mozart, long walks in the country, or candlelit dinners! You are *not* a nonsmoker! And you are *neither* sensitive *nor* caring!"

Drawing by Koren; (c) 1985 The New Yorker Magazine, Inc.

From "Great Pianists Speak for Themselves" by Elyse Mach:

(Firkusny said:) . . . I like to read, especially books about musicians, like the Mozart letters which contain direct references to and ideas about his own music and that of his contemporaries. . . .

. . . . I believe you need as much technique to play a soft note in a Mozart andante as you need for some stormy passage in a Liszt rhapsody. . . .

. . . . I'll always remember the story my old teacher, Suk, told about himself and his entrance into heaven. The first thing he did was go over to Beethoven, drop to his knees, and kiss the composer's hands; he next went over to Wagner and made a deep bow. When he spied Mozart, he ran and hid under a table to that he wouldn't have to admit that he was a composer. If Mozart had such an effect on Suk, what is in store for lesser musicians? Perhaps we won't run and hide provided we have been true to our art.

Paul and Eva Badura-Skoda

Paul was born 1927, in Vienna, studied science and music, graduating from the Vienna Conservatory, concertized widely as a pianist throughout Europe and America. In 1951 he married the concert pianist Eva Halfar born 1929 in Munich, with whom he collaborated in producing scholarly studies of music. In 1966 he and Mrs. Badura-Skoda became professors of music at the University of Wisconsin. After his death his wife retired in Vienna.

From "Interpreting Mozart on the Keyboard" by Eva and Paul Badura-Skoda:

A pianist must be in control and command of his fingers if he is to play Mozart's single melodic lines cantabile and expressively, and give a really even flow ('like oil') to his legato passage-work, which should sound like a melodic line played quickly, and his tingling 'con-brio' passages. For 'non-legato,' which occurs so frequently, the fingers should be kept as curved as possible. One's touch should be clear and sparkling (jeu perle); this is best achieved by slightly drawing in the fingers, so that they tap the keys like little hammers. But here the wrist should always be kept pliable; it should follow the play of the fingers; i.e., in phrasing it should be quite free to take part, just as it should follow the movement of a violin bow. It is particularly important to keep the whole body free of tension, relaxed, shoulders free of strain, the neck muscles relaxed. Mozart's finely developed sense for every kind of naturalness often made him criticize a player's posture:

"All I can say about the daughter of Hamm, the Secretary of War, is that she undoubtedly must have a gift for music, as she has only been learning for three years and yet can play several pieces really well. But I find it difficult to give you an idea of the impression she makes on me when she is playing. She seems to me so curiously affected. She stalks over the clavier with her long, bony fingers in such an odd way—"

(Muzio) Clementi . . . greatly admired Mozart: "I had never before heard anyone play with such spirit and grace."

Clementi's praise is in line with the general opinion of his contemporaries. Dittersdorf* reports a conversation with the Emperor in his autobiography:

Emperor: Have you heard Mozart play?
Dittersdorf: Three times already.
Emperor: Do you like him?
Dittersdorf: Yes; all musicians do.
Emperor: You have heard Clementi, too?
Dittersdorf: Yes.
Emperor: Some prefer him to Mozart, and Greybig is at the head of them. What do you think? Out with it!
Dittersdorf: Clementi's playing is art simply and solely. Mozart's combines art and taste.
Emperor: I said the same.

Like all great creators, Mozart knew how to exploit every expressive resource available in his time. But

---

*Karl Ditters Von Dittersdorf (1739–1799), a native Austrian, was very popular in his day, knew Mozart well, played second violin with Mozart (viola), Haydn (violin) and Wanhals (cello) in at least one 'at home' recital of the quartets Mozart dedicated to Haydn. For most of his life he served as music director for the Prince Bishop of Breslau in Silesia. His operas and concertos show workmanlike ability but lack whatever cachet is required for them to be considered 'great.'

in his day feelings were expressed far more subtly than nowadays, and men's reactions to emotional stimuli were far stronger. One generation will be moved to tears; the next will give an appreciative smile, and the third generation may say, 'A bit pretty-pretty, don't you think?' To draw an analogy: whereas once a smart tap was enough to let loose a flood of feeling, nowadays one often needs a hammer-stroke. There are passages where Mozart could 'make an effect' so that all his listeners were carried away:

> ". . . . just in the middle of the first Allegro there was a passage which I felt sure must please. The audience were quite carried away—and there was a tremendous burst of applause. But as I knew, when I wrote it, what effect it would surely produce, I had introduced the passage again at the close—when there were shouts of 'Da capo!' "

The 'simplicity' which later generations have often held against Mozart is only apparent. His contemporaries were far from finding his music too simple—on the contrary, they found it too complex and varied.

> He is unquestionably one of the greatest original geniuses, and I have never yet met with any composer who had such an amazing wealth of ideas; I could almost wish he were not so lavish in using them. He leaves his hearer out of breath; for hardly has he grasped one beautiful

thought, when another of greater fascination dispels the first, so that in the end it is impossible to retain any of these beautiful melodies, as the composer Dittersdorf wrote about Mozart's compositions.

This 'balance' is indeed one of the main reasons why Mozart-playing presents so many difficulties, despite the simplicity of his musical language. For Mozart had a keen sense of the natural. He rejected all bombast and exaggeration, in fact he got a good deal of amusement from it. This is a bond between him and present-day humanity. (The nineteenth century, with its plush curtains and its love of hollow pathos, found Mozart's directness and naturalness hard to appreciate).

CHARLES ROSEN

(1927–   ), born in New York City, studied at the Juilliard School and at Princeton, and made his concert pianist debut in 1951. He is an accomplished lecturer and writer about music whose *The Classical Style* (1971) won the National Book Award.

From "The Classical Style" by Charles Rosen:

The political ambiance of *Don Giovanni* is given greater weight by the close relation in the eighteenth century between revolutionary thought and eroticism. I have no wish to draw a consistent doctrine from the work, but only to set in relief the significance of some of its aspects. Political and sexual liberalism were intimately connected in the 1780s; even for the most respectable citizens the idea took the shape of a governing fear that republicanism implied complete sexual license. The Marquis de Sade, in his pamphlet *One More Step* did, indeed, claim the most extravagant sexual freedom as a logical corollary of political liberty; his ideas were current everywhere in a milder form, and were the end of an already considerable amount of eighteenth-century speculation. Mozart's early and devoutly Catholic horror at French liberal thought must surely have abated considerably when he became a Freemason, but in any case his personal beliefs have little importance in this connection. The political connotations of sexual liberty were very much alive at the premiere of *Don Giovanni*, and they would have been inescapable. Part of the outrage and the attraction that this work inspired for years to come must be understood in this context. After 1790, the repudiation of sexual liberty and the extreme puritanism of the revolutionary government of France (and of the counter-revolutionary governments elsewhere as well) are a reaction to the intellectual climate that produced *Don Giovanni*, and are reflected in Beethoven's rejection of Mozart's libretti as unworthy of being set to music.

This sense of outrage connected with the opera—and it is implicit in Kierkegaard's view of *Don Giovanni* as the only work that perfectly embodies the essentially erotic nature of music, and in E. T. A. Hoffmann's stressing of what he called its 'romanticism'—this sense of *Don Giovanni* as an attack, at once frontal and oblique, upon aesthetic and moral values is more useful for understanding the opera, and Mozart's music in general, than the common-sense view which shrugs off this aspect impatiently. Music is the most abstract of all the arts only in the sense that it is the least representational; it is, however, the least abstract in its direct physical assault on the listeners' nerves, in the immediacy of effect that its patterns gain from the apparently almost total reduction of mediating symbolism, of all ideas that seem to call for decoding and interpretation, and so to stand between the music and listener. (If, as a matter of fact, the reduction is very far from total, and the listener must expend considerable labor decoding the symbolic relationships set before him, his activity is less conscious, less verbalized, than in any other art.) When this physical immediacy of music is stressed, then its erotic aspect stands well to the fore. Perhaps no composer used the seductive power of music with the intensity and range of Mozart. The flesh is corrupt and corrupting. Behind Kirkegaard's essay on *Don Giovanni* stand the idea that music is a sin: it seems fundamentally sound that he should have chosen Mozart as the most sinful composer of all. What is most extraordinary about Mozart's style is the combination of physical delight—a sensuous play of sonority, an indulgence in the most luscious harmonic sequences—with a purity and economy of line and form that render the seduction all the more efficient.

A more prosaic and more conventionally respectable view of Mozart comes not from the sober perspective of the twentieth century but from the height of Romantic enthusiasm: in the G minor Symphony, a work of passion, violence, and grief for those who love Mozart most, Schumann saw nothing but lightness, grace, and charm. It should be said at once that to reduce a work to the expression of the sentiments, however powerful, is to trivialize it in any case: the G minor Symphony is not much more profound conceived as a tragic cry from the heart than as a work of exquisite charm. Nevertheless, Schumann's attitude to Mozart ends by destroying his vitality as it canonizes him. It is only through recognizing the violence and the sensuality at the center of Mozart's work that we can make a start towards a comprehension of his structures and an insight into his magnificence. In a paradoxical way, however, Schumann's superficial characterizations of the G minor Symphony can help us to see Mozart's daemon more steadily. In all of Mozart's supreme expressions of suffering and terror—the G minor Symphony, *Don Giovanni*, the G minor Quintet, Pamina's aria in *Die Zauberflote*—there is something shockingly voluptuous. Nor does this detract from its power or effectiveness: the grief and the sensuality strengthen each other, and end by becoming indivisible, indistinguishable one from the other. (Tchaikovsky's grief, for example, has an equal lubricity, but his diffuse and wasteful technique of composition makes him far less dangerous.) In his corruption of sentimental values, Mozart is a subversive artist.

Almost all art is subversive: it attacks established

values, and replaces them with those of its own creation; it substitutes its own order for that of society. The disconcertingly suggestive aspects—moral and political—of Mozart's operas are only a surface appearance of this aggression. His works are in many ways an assault upon the musical language that he helped to create: the powerful chromaticism that he could employ with such ease comes near at moments to destroying the tonal clarity that was essential to the significance of his own forms, and it was this chromaticism that had a real influence upon the Romantic style, on Chopin and Wagner in particular. The artistic personality that Haydn created for himself (related to, but not to be confused with, the face he wore for everyday purposes) prevented by its assumption of an easy-going geniality, the full development of the subversive and revolutionary aspect of his art; his music, as E. T. A. Hoffmann wrote, appears to have been composed before original sin. Beethoven's attack was naked, no art was less accomodating in its refusal to accept any other conditions than its own. Mozart was as unaccommodating as Beethoven, and the sheer physical beauty, prettiness, even, of so much of what he composed masks the uncompromising character of his art. It cannot be fully appreciated without recalling the uneasiness and even dismay that it so often evoked in its time, and without recreating in our own mind the conditions in which it could still seem dangerous.

VLADIMIR ASHKENAZY

(1937–) was born in Gorky, U.S.S.R. and is now regarded as an international figure, a much-sought-after concert pianist and conductor. He has recorded concertos of Beethoven, Brahms, Rachmaninoff and Prokofiev as well as most of Mozart, in the latter also serving as orchestral conductor.

From "Great Pianists Speak for Themselves" by Elyse Mach:

(Ashkenazy said:) I wouldn't mind . . . visiting the past if I could just meet some of the classical composers like Beethoven, or Rachmaninoff, or Chopin, or Mozart. I'm not sure whether or not I'd benefit musically from such encounters; to know a man's music you must study the music, not the man, although the composer can be of some help. Yet, I know I'd find the personalities of these men most interesting if for no other reason than to verify what we have heard about them. I'd like to separate legend from fact. Was Beethoven really as eccentric, abrupt, and temperamental as he is made out to be? Rachmaninoff is characterized as a gloomy person, very severe in attitude and appearance. Yet he's one of my favorite composers and, since he was also a great pianist, he could be a fascinating man to observe first-hand. I picture Chopin as a sophisticated, elegant, refined man, perpetually ill, but a genius in spite of it; I would like to see the difficult life of a genius close up. Mozart is very controversial. Some say he was beset with gambling debts and lost a fortune. Yet other accounts of his life disagree with that point. Apparently, he was a disorganized person, especially where his personal affairs were concerned. It certainly doesn't show in his compositions. At any rate, I am curious about their behavior patterns, and I'd like to have my curiosity satisfied.

Ave Atque Vale

Summing up the foregoing opinions and suppositions, what picture emerges? Certainly that of a genius unlike any the world has ever known: a man of earth endowed with abilities granted none other in recorded history. In Shakespearean phrase, take him for all in all, we shall not look upon his like again.

For Mozart, as for all of us, every physical memento of his passage through this life will disappear. In his case the immaterialization is happening with unusual speed. No two likenesses of him seem to represent the same person. The death mask that could have authenticated his features was accidentally dropped by Constanze and broken to bits. Yet plaques, busts, statues and tablets abound in the world. His burial spot is unknown. We still do have a piano or two he is supposed to have owned, some personal trinkets, rings, etc., as well as, in his own hand, hundreds of pages of music autographs and the incomparably frank and brilliant letters. Even to all of these as physical artifacts, we must someday bid goodbye.

But an imperishable monument will always be ours—the transcendent beauty and mystery of his great legacy—the MUSIC.

Bernstein 176
Dittersdorf 184

Rosen 187